THE WAY
PEOPLE
LIVE

Life During the Roaring Twenties

Titles in The Way People Live series include:

THE WAY
PEOPLE
LIVE

Life During the Roaring Twenties

by
Diane Yancey

LUCENT BOOKS
SAN DIEGO, CALIFORNIA

THOMSON
━━━✦━━━ ™
GALE

Detroit • New York • San Diego • San Francisco
Boston • New Haven, Conn. • Waterville, Maine
London • Munich

Library of Congress Cataloging-in-Publication Data

Yancey, Diane.
    Life During the Roaring Twenties / by Diane Yancey.
        p.   cm. — (The way people live)
    Includes bibliographical references and index.
    Summary: Discusses American political, economic, and cultural
life during the nineteen twenties.
    ISBN 1-59018-158-1
    1. United States—Social life and customs—1918–1945—Juvenile
literature.   2. United States—Social conditions—1918–1932—Juvenile
literature.   3. Nineteen twenties—Juvenile literature.   [1. United
States—History—1919–1933.   2. United States—Social life and
customs—1918–1945.   3. Nineteen twenties.]   I. Title.   II. Series.
    E169 .Y34   2002
    973.91'5—dc21

2001007680

Contents

Discovering the Humanity in Us All

Books in The Way People Live series focus on groups of people in a wide variety of circumstances, settings, and time periods. Some books focus on different cultural groups, others, on people in a particular historical time period, while others cover people involved in a specific event. Each book emphasizes the daily routines, personal and historical struggles, and achievements of people from all walks of life.

To really understand any culture, it is necessary to strip the mind of the common notions we hold about groups of people. These stereotypes are the archenemies of learning. It does not even matter whether the stereotypes are positive or negative; they are confining and tight. Removing them is a challenge that's not easily met, as anyone who has ever tried it will admit. Ideas that do not fit into the templates we create are unwelcome visitors—ones we would prefer remain quietly in a corner or forgotten room.

The cowboy of the Old West is a good example of such confining roles. The cowboy was courageous, yet soft-spoken. His time (it is always a he, in our template) was spent alternatively saving a rancher's daughter from certain death on a runaway stagecoach, or shooting it out with rustlers. At times, of course, he was likely to get a little crazy in town after a trail drive, but for the most part, he was the epitome of inner strength. It is disconcerting to find out that the cowboy is human, even a bit childish. Can it really be true that cowboys would line up to help the cook on the trail drive grind coffee, just hoping he would give them a little stick of peppermint candy that came with the coffee shipment? The idea of tough cowboys vying with one another to help "Coosie" (as they called their cooks) for a bit of candy seems silly and out of place.

So is the vision of Eskimos playing video games and watching MTV, living in prefab housing in the Arctic. It just does not fit with what "Eskimo" means. We are far more comfortable with snow igloos and whale blubber, harpoons and kayaks.

Although the cultures dealt with in Lucent's The Way People Live series are often historically and socially well known, the emphasis is on the personal aspects of life. Groups of people, while unquestionably affected by their politics and their governmental structures, are more than those institutions. How do people in a particular time and place educate their children? What do they eat? And how do they build their houses? What kinds of work do they do? What kinds of games do they enjoy? The answers to these questions bring these cultures to life. People's lives are revealed in the particulars and only by knowing the particulars can we understand these cultures' will to survive and their moments of weakness and greatness.

This is not to say that understanding politics does not help to understand a culture. There is no question that the Warsaw ghetto, for example, was a culture that was brought about by the politics and social ideas of Adolf

Hitler and the Third Reich. But the Jews who were crowded together in the ghetto cannot be understood by the Reich's politics. Their life was a day-to-day battle for existence, and the creativity and methods they used to prolong their lives is a vital story of human perseverance that would be denied by focusing only on the institutions of Hitler's Germany. Knowing that children as young as five or six outwitted Nazi guards on a daily basis, that Jewish policemen helped the Germans control the ghetto, that children attended secret schools in the ghetto and even earned diplomas—these are the things that reveal the fabric of life, that can inspire, intrigue, and amaze.

Books in The Way People Live series allow both the casual reader and the student to see humans as victims, heroes, and onlookers. And although humans act in ways that can fill us with feelings of sorrow and revulsion, it is important to remember that "hero," "predator," and "victim" are dangerous terms. Heaping undue pity or praise on people reduces them to objects, and strips them of their humanity.

Seeing the Jews of Warsaw only as victims is to deny their humanity. Seeing them only as they appear in surviving photos, staring at the camera with infinite sadness, is limiting, both to them and to those who want to understand them. To an object of pity, the only appropriate response becomes "Those poor creatures!" and that reduces both the quality of their struggle and the depth of their despair. No one is served by such two-dimensional views of people and their cultures.

With this in mind, The Way People Live series strives to flesh out the traditional, two-dimensional views of people in various cultures and historical circumstances. Using a wide variety of primary quotations—the words not only of the politicians and government leaders, but of the real people whose lives are being examined—each book in the series attempts to show an honest and complete picture of a culture removed from our own by time or space.

By examining cultures in this way, the reader will notice not only the glaring differences from his or her own culture, but also will be struck by the similarities. For indeed, people share common needs—warmth, good company, stability, and affirmation from others. Ultimately, seeing how people really live, or have lived, can only enrich our understanding of ourselves.

Age of Extremes

The 1920s were known as the Lawless Decade, the Flapper Era, and the Jazz Age. They were a period of extremes— a time of Prohibition, Al Capone, flagpole sitters, and marathon dance contests. Everyone talked about a "return to normalcy" after the horrors of World War I (1914–1918), but what they got was ten years of growth, modernization, revelry, and rebellion such as the United States had never seen before. Writer F. Scott Fitzgerald captured the essence of the period when he wrote, "The restlessness approached hysteria. The parties were bigger. The pace was faster, the shows were broader, the buildings were higher, the morals were looser, and the liquor was cheaper."[1]

The Dollar Decade

The "Dollar Decade"—another nickname for the '20s—was a time of exceptional prosperity. Businesses expanded. The stock market soared. Bankers made housing loans and invested in new construction. The majority of people had jobs and went home at night to

---

Normalcy

While running for president in 1920, Warren G. Harding announced that the nation needed "not nostrums [pet schemes for solving problems] but normalcy." Most Americans assumed that meant a return to life as it had been before World War I. The twenties turned out to be anything but normal, as author Lloyd Morris points out in Frank Brookhouser's *These Were Our Years*.

"'Normalcy' was . . . ushered in by the ubiquitous wail of the saxophone. By petting parties and gate crashing. By drunken brawls in exclusive country clubs. By bootleggers and speakeasies; rumrunners, hijacking, bank robberies. By a procession of weeping women eleven blocks long which filed past the mortal remains of [actor] Rudolph Valentino. By the cozy extermination of new enterprisers whose disgruntled competitors took them 'for a ride'. . . . The Federal government fostered a boom in padlocks. Jewelers did a brisk trade in hip flasks. These new accessories were usually made of silver; but one could likewise procure them in gold, sometimes encrusted with gems. For this was the coprosperity era of [Presidents Warren G.] Harding, [Calvin] Coolidge and the luckless [Herbert] Hoover—who foresaw a national destiny of two automobiles in every garage, a fat chicken in every pot. Cooks, bootblacks, clerks, housewives, teachers, errand boys were plunging into the maelstrom [whirlpool] of a runaway bull market in Wall Street."

Flappers kick up their heels during a Charleston dance contest in 1926.

houses with electric lights, telephones, flush toilets, and built-in bathtubs. "Electric lighting is so much a matter of course today that it is hard to recover [remember] the days before its advent,"[2] said one observer.

Not everyone was able to enjoy the good times. Crop prices were so low that many farmers went bankrupt. Millions of blacks and poor immigrants struggled against discrimination and poverty. In the rural South and in mill and mining towns, work was backbreaking, wages were low, and unemployment was common. Help from private charities and social service organizations was limited since most Americans believed that anyone could get

ahead with a little hard work. The prevailing philosophy was "People in actual need must be helped, because 'you wouldn't let a *dog* starve,' but we must not make it too easy for them!"[3]

The poor themselves had high hopes that their lives were going to get better. After all, with new modern means of financing, they were able to afford a down payment on a car or a radio. And people who were well informed assured them that prosperity would soon include everyone. "A chicken in every pot, and two cars in every garage,"[4] promised Herbert Hoover in his 1928 presidential campaign. In view of the economic boom, few doubted that his words were coming true.

Small-Town Values, Upside Down

One of the signs that things were getting better was that more Americans had time for fun and frivolity. In big cities like Chicago, Detroit, and New York, the fun seemed better if it skirted close to danger. People went to speakeasies (illegal bars), drank bootleg gin, and danced the Charleston until dawn. Values seemed turned upside down. Youth were modern and independent. The older generation was out of touch. Police were corrupt. Gangsters were admired for their bigger-than-life style. "It is a strange commentary upon our system of law and justice,"[5] the *Chicago Tribune* remarked, referring to the lavish funeral of Chicago's first gang leader, "Big Jim" Colosimo, in 1920. The hoodlum's pallbearers included three judges, a congressman, and an assistant state attorney who marched shoulder to shoulder with racketeers and brothel owners.

While the twenties roared in the cities, the rest of the country was more sane and sensible. "Monday evening we went over to a little club we belong to where we play cards every week," explained one young lawyer. "Tuesday we went to that lecture for the benefit of the Day Nurs-

Despite the raucous behavior going on in the big cities during the twenties, many people across the country enjoyed wholesome pastimes like listening to the radio.

In small towns across the country, the twenties remained a time of family values and wholesome pastimes. Parents were accessible. Children were carefree. In *These Were Our Years*, historian and author Frank Brookhouser describes this almost-overlooked aspect of the decade.

"The day seemed to stretch ahead endlessly when a boy awakened then.

There was fun in school. There were boys to talk baseball with. There were favorite girls to see and admire and perhaps wish for.

After school there would be baseball on the street or up in the field, the 'pick up sides' kind.

And then there was dinner, although it was always called supper in our town.

After supper, with Dad home from work and weary, there would be a brief period of rest on the front porch.

But Dad never stayed tired for long . . . and in a short time he would say, 'Want to toss a few before it gets dark?'

And the two of them, father and son, would get out on the front lawn and throw some to each other, the son telling the father what a good glove it was that he had received for Christmas.

The darkness brought new games with the gang, Pump Pump Pull Away across the street or Run Sheep Run around the block.

And, finally, when the boy was tired and sweaty and happy, it was time for going to bed. And it was amazing how short the day had been.

That was the way some of us were in those years."

---

ery, Wednesday I forget what we did, but we went somewhere or other—and so the week goes."[6] Values here were conservative and family oriented. People took part in community activities, voted on election day, and went to church on Sunday. Most parents wanted their children to get a good education and worried that their teens were becoming rebellious. "I'm going to bring my little girl up just as strict as I can," said one mother, "then if she does go bad I won't feel that I haven't done my duty."[7]

Crazy and Corrupt

A mixture of flamboyance and conservatism, the Roaring Twenties were more than just the raucous, happy-go-lucky times depicted in books and movies. One historian writes,

On the surface, the 1920s were joyous years—the years of the Sunday drive and the big football weekend, the raccoon coat, the speakeasy. . . . But this was only on the surface. The '20s were also a time when tens of millions of Americans . . . felt profoundly alienated from the society in which they lived. Looking back on the decade, the nation seemed close to falling apart.[8]

It fell apart on October 29, 1929. The crash of the stock market ushered in the Great Depression, followed by World War II and new generations who could only wonder how such a decade of extremes came to be. As one observer said, "A calamity gave it birth, and a calamity ended it. It was a decade of giants, like none before or since."[9]

Crazy Consumption

Americans entered the twenties wanting less government in their lives. During World War I, the Railroad Administration had regulated railroads. The Fuel Administration had monitored coal supplies and gasoline consumption. The National War Labor Board had worked to resolve disputes between management and labor to keep production high. At the urging of the Food Administration, everyone had observed "meatless Mondays," "wheatless Wednesdays," and other measures to help the soldiers overseas.

By war's end, people were tired of all the regulations and sacrifice. They wanted the freedom to concentrate on their own affairs. They also wanted to be able to enjoy the pleasures of life—traveling, modernizing their homes, or going out for an evening of entertainment. The Republicans, who supported small government and private enterprise, looked like the ones to give them such opportunities. In 1920, Republican Warren G. Harding was elected president of the United States, not because of his expertise but because he seemed to have no desire to interfere in people's lives. "America's present need is not heroics but healing . . . not revolution but restoration,"[10] he assured the public.

A Celebration of Business

Harding was hardworking and sincere, but his limited talents led him to choose dishonest men to help run the country. His administration was marked by corruption and scandal, the most infamous of which was the Teapot Dome affair. In 1923, the public learned that Secretary of the Interior Albert Fall had secretly leased government oil fields to private oil companies in exchange for cash. On August 2 of that year, however, a disillusioned Harding had died in office of a heart attack. He was succeeded by Vice President Calvin Coolidge.

Coolidge, a scrupulously honest man, also believed that government should play the smallest role possible in American life. As president, he was probusiness, and his goal was to make sure that he did nothing to hamper the growth of the economy. "The business of America is business,"[11] Coolidge declared

Vice President Calvin Coolidge (right) became president in 1923 after Republican Warren G. Harding (left) died in office.

A country drive in a Ford Model T.

in 1925 as he cut government, discouraged Congress from passing regulatory laws, and did everything else he could to encourage private enterprise.

With Coolidge and the Republicans leading the country, American business flourished. New industries were formed and old ones expanded. Many business owners generously introduced policies that benefited their employees. The Bausch and Lomb optical company began offering free eye exams and dental clinics. Ford Motor Company shortened its workweek and introduced paid vacations. U.S. Steel cut its workday from twelve to eight hours and raised wages.

Some employers offered their workers the chance to buy stock in their companies at below-market values. This was seen as a valuable benefit since the stock market was continuously rising during the twenties. People believed stock was a good buy and were eager to own shares because, in the new prosperity, they were sure the value would go up.

The Family Car

The automobile was the definitive symbol of national prosperity in the twenties. "Why on earth do you need to study what's changing this country?" one man asked. "I can tell you what's happening in just four letters: A-U-T-O."[12]

Henry Ford had marketed his first Model T in 1908 for $850, a hefty price in those days, but by 1926 the price had dropped to about $300. The reason for the drop was Ford's use of standardized interchangeable parts and an assembly line system—a conveyer that carried the frame of the car past workers who each added a part. Ford installed his first assembly line in Detroit, Michigan, in 1914, and soon cars could be assembled in about an hour and a half. (Earlier processes took about fourteen hours.) The cut in time resulted in a huge reduction in production costs, and thus a reduction in price.

Suddenly, people who never dreamed of owning a car could afford one. Almost everyone bought one, even if they had to borrow money to do so. One small-town banker observed, "The paramount ambition of the average man a few years ago was to own a home and have a bank account. The ambition of the same man today is to own a car."[13]

For many, a car was a symbol of social and financial success. For others, it symbolized freedom and family values. "We don't spend anything on recreation except for the car. We save everyplace we can and put the money into the car. It keeps the family together,"[14] explained one woman.

Tin Lizzie

In 1921, Americans bought 1.5 million cars, and the majority of them were Fords. Boxy, temperamental, and available only in black, the Model T—also known as a flivver, a Tin Lizzie, or "the jalopy"—was the butt of many jokes, but most were affectionate ones like the following:

"Can I sell you a speedometer?"
"I don't use one. When my Ford is running five miles an hour, the fender rattles; twelve miles an hour my teeth rattle, and fifteen miles an hour the transmission drops out."[15]

There was good reason for the jokes. The Model T joggled and shook its passengers un-

mercifully (although unpaved, deeply rutted roads were part of the problem, too). It was also hard to start in the cold. If it lacked a self-starter, and many did, the owner had to crank it by hand in order to get the engine to fire. One girl remembered,

We'd all pile into the T for a ride, five kids and Mumma, and Dad would crank. We all just sat there and held our breath, waiting and hoping, and Dad would crank and crank and crank. A lot of times I was worried Dad might drop dead from cranking. But then after awhile the motor would start up and everyone would holler and cheer.[16]

Because the crank had a tendency to kick back, many owners suffered broken arms and sprained wrists in addition to sore shoulders.

The Tin Lizzie lacked all but the basics. "You didn't have a heater or a defroster in the T," one man remembered. "My father carried . . . a little bag of salt. He'd rub the salt on the windshield every now and then, and in winter he'd have about an inch of eyespace to see through."[17] The engine also frequently overheated. The car could not get up hills unless it had a running start, and many people discovered that due to its mechanical shortcomings it went uphill better in reverse than forward.

Still, the Model T had numerous advantages. As one Ford advertisement claimed, it was "designed for everyday wear and tear."[18] It could go anywhere, and was simple to repair. Most breakdowns could be fixed with baling wire, hairpins, or chewing gum. The Model T was also versatile. For instance, if a farmer replaced the car's back tires with tractor tires, he could use it to pull a plow.

Despite the existence of other makes of cars such as Locomobile, Premier, Peerless,

Few Americans imagined the widespread effect the automobile would have on society, affecting such diverse aspects of life as family vacations, the growth of the suburbs, and teen sex. In *Only Yesterday: An Informal History of the 1920's*, historian Frederick Lewis Allen reviews other changes brought about by the growing popularity of the car.

Automobiles filled the roads of New York City by 1925.

"As [the automobile] came, it changed the face of America. . . . Villages on Route 61 bloomed with garages, filling stations, hot-dog stands, chicken-dinner restaurants, tea-rooms, tourists' rests, camping sites, and affluence. . . . Railroad after railroad gave up its branch lines, or saw its revenues slowly dwindling under the competition of mammoth interurban busses and trucks snorting along six-lane concrete highways. The whole country was covered with a network of passenger bus-lines. In thousands of towns, at the beginning of the decade a single traffic officer at the junction of Main Street and Central Street had been sufficient for the control of traffic. By the end of the decade, what a difference!—red and green lights, blinkers, one-way streets, boulevard stops, stringent and yet more stringent parking ordinances—and still a shining flow of traffic that backed up for blocks along Main Street every Saturday and Sunday afternoon. Slowly but surely the age of steam was yielding to the gasoline age."

Chrysler, and Studebaker, the Model T was a top seller until General Motors introduced its Chevrolet in a variety of models and colors and at irresistibly low prices. Then, in order to compete, Ford brought out his new Model A version in 1927. Americans now had an abundance of affordable choices when it came to transportation. They could have a two-door phaeton (an open car that seated five), a sporty roadster, a sedan, or a pickup. They could also choose from a variety of colors, including Niagara blue and Arabian sand. One historian comments, "The new models constituted an absorbing topic of conversation. Throngs visited the [car] shows, discussing the merits of sleeve valves, free wheeling, air cooling, [and] the number of cylinders from fours to twelves and sixteens."[19]

On the Road

As the auto industry boomed, so did support industries—steel, rubber, glass, and oil, all essential ingredients in car manufacturing. The boom provided millions of jobs, not only for those who played a role in building cars but those who operated taxis, buses, and trucking lines. Jobs designing traffic lights and parking lots also increased.

Highway construction firms and asphalt and cement companies worked overtime as people demanded more roads, wider roads, and paved roads that would not become mud bogs when it rained. "Filling stations" sprang up at regular intervals to supply the need for fuel. Repair shops sprouted everywhere. Roadside cafés offered hot meals to travelers, although many carried their own picnic lunches.

As more families began to take to the road for vacations, enterprising individuals set up tourist camps. The camps ranged from grassy fields where anyone could pitch a tent to facilities that included private cabins, hot water, cooking stoves, and pit toilets. Some people who had extra space in their homes offered beds and meals for passersby who

Workmen flatten and pave a road in a housing division. Road and highway construction boomed in the twenties as automobile use became widespread.

needed a place to stay. Most of these facilities were comfortable; some were not. "A Tourist Home by any other name still adds up to a boarding house,"[20] stated one traveler.

America, a Consumer Society

The automobile industry was not the only segment of business to prosper in the '20s. Manufacturers and merchandisers began to realize that people were consumers, so they started turning out a multitude of products for them to buy—everything from mouthwash and wristwatches to bedroom furniture and bathroom fixtures. People bought enthusiastically, because they needed things, they wanted to keep up with their neighbors, and just for the sheer fun of it. In case they paused to doubt the wisdom of their spending sprees, they were urged to keep spending. "The American citizen's first importance to his country is no longer that of a citizen but that of consumer. Consumption is a new necessity," one newspaper editorialized. "The way to make business boom is to buy."[21]

A feeling of "gotta have it" pervaded the country. People felt that if their neighbors were able to buy pianos, toasters, new sofas, and the like, they ought to be able to do so as well. Needs and wants often exceeded income, however, so people had to find the extra money to make ends meet. Business had an answer to that, too: credit.

Making payments on a house was a common practice at the time, but buying consumer goods on credit was a new concept in the '20s. Those who tried it, however, found it delightfully easy. A small down payment let them take the article home. Payments plus interest could be made over the next several years.

Consumers liked credit buying because it was a way of getting what they wanted

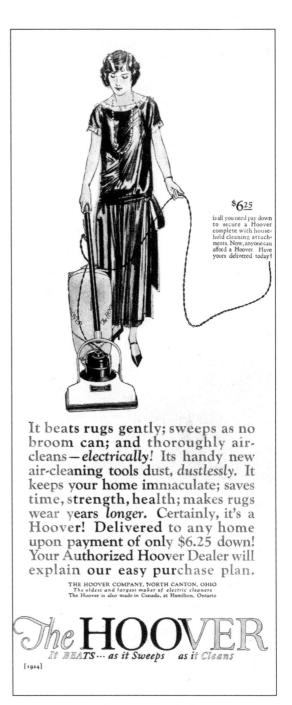

It beats **rugs gently; sweeps** as no **broom can; and thoroughly air-cleans** — *electrically!* Its handy new **air-cleaning tools** dust, *dustlessly.* It keeps **your home immaculate; saves time, strength, health;** makes rugs wear **years** *longer.* Certainly, it's a **Hoover! Delivered** to any home upon **payment of only $6.25 down!** **Your Authorized Hoover Dealer will explain our easy purchase plan.**

THE HOOVER COMPANY, NORTH CANTON, OHIO
The oldest and largest maker of electric cleaners
The Hoover is also made in Canada, at Hamilton, Ontario

The HOOVER
It BEATS··· as it Sweeps as it Cleans
[1924]

$6.25 is all you need pay down to secure a Hoover complete with household cleaning attachments. Now, anyone can afford a Hoover. Have yours delivered today!

A 1924 Hoover advertisement beckons to consumers discovering credit.

Not everyone benefited from the good times in the twenties. In *Babbitts and Bohemians: The American 1920s*, Elizabeth Stevenson describes the boll weevil, one of the biggest problems experienced by people in the South.

"For the South, the decade of the twenties was the boll-weevil decade. By 1922 the little snout-nosed beetle covered the entire southeastern cotton-producing region to its northern limits. It had been on its way since the fall of 1894, when the first occurrence in the United States was noticed just over the line from Mexico to Brownsville, Texas. It had reached Louisiana in 1903, Mississippi in 1907, and Georgia in 1916. Its effect was as all-encompassing as an Egyptian plague. Losses were 'from one-third to one-half of the yield. . . . Farmers, merchants, and bankers were bankrupted; farms and homes in whole communities were deserted; labor and tenants were demoralized and moved to other sections; and a general feeling of panic and fear followed the boll weevil as it moved into locality after locality.' Songs were sung about this disaster; babies of tenant farmers were named Weevil."

without having to wait for it. Businessmen liked credit buying because they could sell more goods. "The rise and spread of the dollar-down-and-so-much-per plan extends credit for virtually everything—homes, $200 overstuffed living-room suites, electric washing machines, automobiles, fur coats, diamond rings—to persons of whom frequently little is known as to their intention or ability to pay,"[22] reported one observer in 1925.

Some conservatives warned that the misuse of credit buying could spell disaster for the unwise spender. People who overspent were, in the words of one banker, "mortgaging future earnings for the gratification of present-day pleasures,"[23] with possibly disastrous results. Most people did not choose to listen. They preferred to yield to the coaxing of salesmen who urged them to "enjoy while you pay." Being in debt came to be seen as a laughing matter. One standard joke had a husband remarking to his wife, "One more payment and the furniture is ours," to which she replies, "Good. Then we can throw it out and get some new stuff."[24]

Chains

Not only were there more things to buy than in the past, there were more and better places to shop as well. "The Busy Bee Bazaar and the Temple of Economy on Main Street are being displaced by brisk, competing men's wear, women's wear, electrical, gift, leather-goods, and other 'specialty' shops. A swarm of chain stores is pressing hard upon the small independent retailer,"[25] reported observers in a midwestern town in 1925.

In the favorable business climate, chain stores—networks of stores owned by the same person or company—spread from coast to coast. American shoppers found that Woolworth, J.C. Penney, Piggly Wiggly, or Western Auto had many advantages over a small family-owned business that had been the norm in earlier decades. The chains offered a wider selection of products. Sometimes they offered better service. Their prices were lower because they purchased goods in large amounts and at low cost. The savings could thus be passed on to the customer. One author writes,

"Mrs. Smith no longer patronized her 'nabor-hood' store; she climbed into her . . . car to drive to the red-fronted chain grocery and save twenty-seven cents on her daily purchases."[26] By 1929, almost half of all grocery sales were through chain stores.

The High Calling of Salesmen

When people stepped through the doors of a furniture store or a car dealership, their desire to buy was encouraged by salesmen. Salesmanship—the way a salesman approached the customer, described the product, and persuaded the customer to buy—was as important as the quality of the product itself.

Author Sinclair Lewis defined salesmanship as "a cosmic purpose . . . not of selling anything in particular, for or to anybody in particular, but pure Selling."[27]

Not every man instinctively knew how to be a top-notch salesman. Courses were offered in "scientific salesmanship," in which salesmen could learn the psychology and techniques needed to "close a deal." Books on salesmanship were also popular. A best-seller of the time was *The Man Nobody Knows* by Bruce Barton. Barton's book portrays Jesus Christ as a businessman who gathered a group of top-notch salesmen as his disciples and taught them how to "sell" God's message to humankind. "He picked up twelve men from the bottom ranks of business and forged

Montgomery Ward was just one of the many chain stores that became popular in the twenties.

them into an organization that conquered the world,"[28] Barton pointed out.

Even with training, being a successful salesman was hard work. Companies set quotas for their employees to meet each month, and only by pressuring customers could that quota be met. One Ford dealer in a small town explained his company's techniques: "I am willing to confess that we rode the public a little ourselves while we were getting rid of our big surplus of cars. There are always some people that you can sell anything to if you hammer them hard enough. We had a salesman named Nichols who was a humdinger at running down prospects."[29]

One company took practical, but humiliating, steps to motivate its salesmen to make their quotas. At the annual company banquet, the best salesman was served an elaborate and enormous dinner. The next best salesman earned a dinner with one less item on his plate, and so on down the line. The worst salesman sat in embarrassment with a small plate of boiled beans and a couple of crackers as his portion.

Because of all the hype, many American men came to believe that the term "good businessman" was the highest compliment one could give or receive. Good business practices equaled success, and could be applied to everything. For instance, a young man sang the praises of his family minister by saying, "He always wound up his sermons at quarter to twelve . . . and he always wound them up with a bang, too. . . . He had the actor's instinct to quit while they still want more. He was a real business man."[30]

To some salesmen, their work was almost a religious calling. They became involved in booster clubs, so called because they aimed to

The Divine Salesman

In a decade when business was king, salesmanship became an art and salesmen aspired to become the best. At the top was Bruce Barton, who wrote the best-seller *The Man Nobody Knows* in 1924. In it, Barton argues that Jesus was the world's greatest salesman. A portion of his work is included in *This Fabulous Century*, edited by Ezra Bowen.

"He [Jesus] would be a national advertiser today, I am sure, as he was the great advertiser of his own day. Take any one of the parables, no matter which—you will find that it exemplifies all the principles on which advertising text books are written.

1. First of all they are marvelously condensed, as all good advertising must be. Jesus hated prosy dullness.

2. His language was marvelously simple—a second great essential. All the great things in human life are one-syllable things—love, joy, hope, home, child, wife, trust, faith, God.

3. Sincerity glistened like sunshine through every sentence he uttered. The advertisements which persuade people to act are written by men who have an abiding respect for the intelligence of their readers, and a deep sincerity regarding the merits of the goods they have to sell.

4. Finally he knew the necessity for repetition and practiced it. No important truth can be impressed upon the minds of any large number of people by being said only once."

Salesmen line up next to their cars at Gehl Brothers Manufacturing Company in Wisconsin in 1921. The art of salesmanship was elevated to new heights during the twenties.

boost the interests of local business and the community. These clubs included Rotary, the Kiwanis, the Elks, and the Lions Club. In addition to social events, members did charitable work such as providing the blind with white canes, distributing Christmas gifts to poor children, and giving money to the Boy Scouts. "Rotary and its big ideal of Service is my religion," said one midwesterner. "I have gotten more out of it than I ever got out of church."[31]

Will You Buy?

A salesman could not push all merchandise. Food, laundry soap, cigarettes, and similar goods usually sat on a grocery store shelf until someone came in to buy. Advertising was the answer to this kind of marketing difficulty. "Advertising is to a business what fertil-

izer is to a farm,"[32] one midwestern paper pointed out.

In the past, advertising had been low-key, with products described in a sober, factual manner. "P&G Naphtha Soap: The White Naphtha Soap in the Blue Wrapper,"[33] one advertisement said. Beginning in the '20s, advertisers began to appeal to the public's emotions, to persuade them that they needed to buy products if they were going to be healthy, look young and attractive, or make their lives more carefree. For instance, one ad for a laundry service promised more leisure time: "Time for sale! Will you buy? . . . Right in your city, you can purchase tomorrows. Time for youth and beauty! Time for club work, for church and community activities. Time for books and plays and concerts. Time for home and children."[34]

There was no escaping the advertising— it was in newspapers, in magazines, and on the radio. Sometimes it rained down as coupons, dropped from a small plane. Sometimes it was written boldly in the air by skywriters. Fortunately, people loved it. They enjoyed learning about the latest products, and they also appreciated its entertainment value. Some of the most successful ads were unique, like the Burma-Shave signs that appeared every few hundred yards along a stretch of highway, luring motorists to buy shaving cream. A first sign might ask, "Does your husband." A few hundred yards farther on came the next message, "Misbehave." Then came

"Grunt and Grumble," and "Rant and Rave?" Another short stint brought the startling phrase, "Shoot the Brute some," and finally, to everyone's delight, the surprise finish— "Burma-Shave."[35]

Some advertisers took a more serious tone. They based their ads on "snob appeal" and had a famous person give a testimonial about the excellence of the product. "Princesse Marie de Bourbon of Spain tells how she cares for her flower-like skin,"[36] said one ad for Pond's cold cream. Millions of women felt like royalty when they massaged

A 1923 advertisement on a metal serving tray.

the cold cream into their faces every night.

Other advertisements played on the public's fears. One of the best of these was an ad for Listerine showing a somber young woman under the heading "Often a Bridesmaid but never a Bride." The text of the ad read, "Most of the girls in her set [age group] were married or about to be. And as her birthdays crept gradually toward that tragic thirty mark, marriage seemed farther from her life than ever. You, yourself, rarely know when you have halitosis (unpleasant breath)."[37]

Some advertisements promised miraculous improvements in health or body shape. Some offered mail-order lessons to help one learn to draw or play the piano. Other ads used pictures of attractive women to sell everything from stockings to electric washing machines. "We grew up founding our dreams on the infinite promises of American advertising," said F. Scott Fitzgerald's wife, Zelda. "I still believe that one can learn to play the piano by mail and that mud will give you a perfect complexion."[38]

Unfortunately, no one paid attention to whether advertisements were truthful or not. It seemed perfectly reasonable that Lucky Strike cigarettes could make a person slim and Fleischmann's yeast could cure constipation and acne. People took it for granted that their toothpaste fought gum disease when in fact it contained an ingredient that could kill. Most buyers did not even question advertisers who made up new diseases such as halitosis, bromodosis (odor caused by foot perspiration), and homotosis (a lack of nice furniture) in order to sell their products as cures.

New Phenomenon

From advertising to automobiles, credit buying to chain stores, the economy was changing. So, too, were other aspects of American society, from the food people put on the dinner table to the way they viewed the institution of marriage. Much of the change could be attributed to the fact that America was becoming an urban society. One historian points out, "For the first time in American history, according to the census bureau, more people were living in cities than in the countryside and villages combined."[39]

The nation was shifting into a new era. The move was unsettling, overwhelming, and ultimately transforming.

Thoroughly Modern

For America, the 1920s marked the point in time when the country began developing into a modern society. Attitudes, opportunities, and activities changed. The automobile replaced the horse and buggy. Women got the vote. Small towns grew into cities, and big cities expanded as people moved in from the country in hopes of finding better jobs and getting ahead in life.

Thousands of the urban newcomers were blacks who left the South to escape social and economic oppression. They settled in northern cities such as Detroit, Philadelphia, Pittsburgh, Chicago, and New York. One man remembered, "Everybody came to Chicago. There was a tremendous need for unskilled labor at the stockyards, for porters in the hotels and for redcaps [porters] at the railroad stations. And these were good jobs, better than what black folks had in the South. So they migrated by the thousands, like my family."[40]

Blacks and whites who abandoned their farms for the city often discovered that they had simply traded one kind of hardship for another. Some regretted the move. "We thought we'd have an easier time when we moved in from the farm three years ago, but now my husband is laid off and can't get work anywhere," one woman reported. "The boy is still working, but we never know anything about him any more. . . . He might be better if we had stayed on the farm, but I suppose he'd be in town all the time anyway."[41] Most were philosophical about the difficulties,

however, and remained optimistic that, with all the opportunities at hand, their new life would soon get better.

New Life for Women

Men remained the head of the household and the breadwinner in the family during the twenties, but women's roles and opportunities changed significantly. The Nineteenth Amendment, giving women the right to vote beginning in 1920, was empowering, as one woman recalls:

> I remember the first time my mother ever voted. It was when Al Smith was running against Herbert Hoover [in 1928]. As it turned out, my father voted for one of them and my mother voted for the other. My father said to her, "Don't you realize that you are simply canceling out my vote?" Mother knew it, of course, but that didn't stop her.[42]

Inspired by their new independence and power, some women went out and got jobs. Few had worked outside the home before the war, and when they had, their choices had been limited to teaching, nursing, or secretarial jobs. In the twenties, women entered new fields. Many found work as salespersons or opened their own tearooms and beauty shops. Some began selling real estate. Others found positions in publishing and advertising.

As thousands of blacks began new lives in northern cities, they looked for leaders to encourage, represent, and help bolster their pride in their race. Radical, Jamaican-born Marcus Garvey seemed a qualified role model to many—until he was convicted for mail fraud in 1925. The following excerpt, included in Peter Jennings and Todd Brewster's *The Century*, gives the highlights of Garvey's message.

"Marcus Garvey preached the spirit of pan-Africanism [the belief that all persons of African heritage should unite to achieve common objectives] and described a new African-American identity, more African than American. . . . A hundred thousand people joined Garvey's Universal Negro Improvement Association [UNIA], which stood in direct contrast to the older and more established National Association for the Advancement of Colored People. And for each person with a membership in UNIA, there were hundreds more who joined Garvey in spirit.

Garvey opposed interracial marriage and looked upon light-skinned blacks as inferior. His newspaper, *The Negro World*, preached separatism and refused advertisements for skin lighteners and hair straighteners. Garvey declared that Christ was black, indeed that all civilization had sprung from the black peoples of North Africa, and his solution to America's race dilemma was the return of black Americans to Africa. Few Harlemites followed his message to the extreme, but with both the revival of the Klan and the race riots of 1919 very much in mind, the theme of black pride attracted them enormously."

Black pride leader Marcus Garvey (center) leaves court in handcuffs after being convicted of mail fraud.

Suffragettes celebrate passage of the Nineteenth Amendment, granting women the right to vote in 1920.

With a second member of the family contributing to the household budget, couples had more money to spend. Many modernized their homes and installed central heating and indoor plumbing. Many more purchased the latest laborsaving devices—washing machines, electric irons, kitchen ranges, refrigerators, and vacuum cleaners. The improvements freed them from backbreaking routines such as washing clothes on a washboard and chopping wood for the stove that had once taken up so much of their free time. One woman testified,

I have felt better since I worked than ever before in my life. I get up at five-thirty.

My husband takes his dinner and the boys buy theirs uptown and I cook supper. We have an electric washing machine, electric iron, and vacuum sweeper. I don't even have to ask my husband any more because I buy these things with my own money. I bought an icebox last year—a big one that holds 125 pounds.[43]

Advances in Health

Not only were women feeling better in the twenties, they were living longer. So were men. In 1920, the average life expectancy was fifty-five. By 1930, it was sixty. The gain was the largest ever made in a decade.

There were practical reasons for the improvement. Newly established public health services were improving sanitation and controlling communicable diseases. Water supplies were being cleaned up, so typhoid and other waterborne infections were dropping. People still treated their ailments with patent medicines such as Tonsiline ("The National Sore Throat Remedy") and Mother Gray's Sweet Powders ("Benefit many children complaining of Headaches, Colds, Feverishness, Worms, Stomach Troubles and other irregu-larities"),[44] but an increasing number went to well-trained doctors and modern hospitals. In the cities, patients benefited from the services of specialists who were able to diagnose and treat conditions that would have puzzled a general practitioner twenty years before.

People were also healthier because they were eating better. Magazines such as the *Ladies Home Journal* and *Good Housekeeping* impressed their readers with the benefits of fruits and vegetables, and women served their families more of these foods. In addition, modern processing techniques made it easier for people to buy and eat everything

A doctor administers the Schick test to Health Department employees to determine whether they are susceptible to diphtheria.

from canned pineapple to tinned ox-tongue all year round. Prices were affordable, too. "Canned goods you buy today are so good that it isn't worth your while to do so much,"[45] one homemaker said to justify the fact that she did little home canning anymore.

Convenience foods ranged from Wonder bread to Kool-aid. Several types of breakfast cereals became available, including Rice Krispies and Wheaties. People also enjoyed Kraft's Velveeta cheese spread for the first time, along with homogenized milk, Hormel canned ham, Oscar Mayer wieners, and Peter Pan peanut butter. Despite the new abundance of candy snacks—Butterfingers, Reese's Peanut Butter Cups, Almond Roca, and the Baby Ruth bar, to name a few—the general health of the nation still improved.

There were two groups, however, who did not benefit from better nutrition: the poor, who could afford only the cheapest foods such as potatoes, beans, and inexpensive cuts of meat, and young women who were trying to achieve a stylishly slim figure. Counting calories was popular in the twenties, and the advent of the bathroom scale allowed girls to track their weight better than before. Some young women went to dangerous lengths to be thin, as one doctor noted: "A strikingly sad example of improper dieting was the case of a shapely motion-picture actress, who became a nervous wreck and blasted her career by restricting herself to tomatoes, spinach and orange juice."[46]

Psychology Craze

Women and men of the '20s were not only interested in their own physical well-being, they were fascinated by anything that related to their mental health as well. They were particularly intrigued by the newfangled notion of psychology, the study of behavior and the mind. Books dealing with psychology were sure sellers, and popular titles included *The Psychology of Golf, The Psychology of Selling Life Insurance, Ten Thousand Dreams Interpreted,* and *Sex Problems Solved.* The latter two were available through the Sears Roebuck catalog.

The theories of Sigmund Freud, the founder of psychoanalysis, were all the rage, and even ordinary people used words like "Freudian," "ego," "defense mechanism," and "repressed" in casual conversation. Because many of Freud's theories were complex, however, journalists often simplified them so that the reader received one basic message: Sex

The theories of Sigmund Freud, founder of psychoanalysis, were at the forefront of a psychology craze in the twenties.

was the prime force that motivated human behavior. Everything one thought, said, or did stemmed from some sexual impulse. One author wrote, "If you were patriotic or liked the violin, you were in the grip of sex—in a sublimated [subconscious] form. The first requirement of mental health was to have an uninhibited sex life. If you would be well and happy, you must obey your libido [sex instinct]."[47]

At cocktail parties and intellectual gatherings, sex was an openly discussed topic, so much so that F. Scott Fitzgerald wrote, "By 1926 the universal pre-occupation with sex had become a nuisance."[48] The term "sex appeal" was used to describe the attraction men had for women and vice versa. In 1921, people read with shocked delight about the first Miss America beauty pageant and its bevy of sexy contestants in one-piece swimsuits.

Magazines, books, plays, and movies were filled with sexual references. For instance, in Theodore Dreiser's *An American Tragedy*, the author describes a couple's first sexual episode in what was then considered shocking prose: "The thing was done, a wild convulsive pleasure motivating both, so much more of a paradise than either might ever know again."[49] Dreiser's book was banned by city authorities in Boston. Actress Mae West's play *Sex* was more explicit and had the distinction of being shut down in open-minded New York City. West was put on trial and served ten days in jail for putting on an indecent show.

Better "to Be a Divorcee than to Be an Old Maid"

With a renewed interest in sex and psychology, women began to evaluate their marriages. Many decided they were unwilling to continue in relationships that were abusive,

boring, or otherwise not working. An advice columnist of the time explained:

> The reason there are more divorces is that people are demanding more of life than they used to. Grandmother had to stand grandpa, for he was her meal ticket and her card of admission to good society. . . . Now we view the matter differently. We see that no good purpose is achieved by keeping two people together who have come to hate each other.[50]

One out of six marriages failed in the '20s, up from one out of seventeen in 1890. Two-thirds of all breakups were initiated by the wife, and divorce lost some of the stigma it had had in the past. A divorced woman was often seen as modern, daring, and even more attractive. Young women got married more casually than before and tended to have the attitude of one New Yorker who said, "It would be much more exciting to be a divorcee than to be an old maid."[51]

Bringing Up Baby

For couples who married, better birth-control techniques allowed them to have smaller families than in the past. Middle-class couples often had three or four children, rather than the six to fourteen that their parents had borne and raised. The less-educated poor continued to have large families, and poor women often died in childbirth and from illegal abortions, motivating reformist Margaret Sanger to pioneer one of the first national birth-control movements. "It is imperative Mr. President, that as a nation the United States meet the problem of an uncontrollable birth rate,"[52] she wrote to Coolidge in 1925. The president ignored her plea.

Actress Mae West in a scene from the play Sex. *The play was shut down by police; West was tried and convicted for putting on an indecent show.*

When it came to child rearing, some progressive women were fascinated with the theories of psychologist John B. Watson, whose motto was "Man is a machine." Watson was a behavioralist, one who believed that environment was the most important factor in influencing behavior and forming a child's character. He stated, "Give me a dozen healthy infants . . . and I'll guarantee to take any one at random and train him to be any type of specialist I might select—doctor, lawyer, artist, merchant."[53]

Watson's beliefs translated into advice that sounds bizarre and even cruel today. Parents were told to avoid "smothering" their children with too much attention and affection. Children should never be hugged or kissed, Watson maintained, and they should never be allowed to sit on their mother's lap. They should be fed according to a strict schedule and should learn early on that crying for attention would not work. "No woman knows enough to raise a child,"[54] Watson stated.

Watson's theories were so popular that the Department of Labor incorporated many of them into an infant and child care pamphlet. Nevertheless, most women continued to raise their children in more traditional ways, singing them lullabies at night, playing with them, helping them with their homework, and ensuring that their physical and emotional needs were well met.

A Good Education

Children and young people in the 1920s had more opportunities to get an education than did youth in earlier generations. Child labor was less common, and educators pushed for compulsory school attendance up to the age of fourteen or even higher. Many parents seconded the schools' efforts, making statements such as "We want them [our children] to have a good education so they can get along easier than their father," and "If they don't have a good education, they'll never know anything but hard work."[55]

By the end of the decade, educators had achieved their goal of mandatory school attendance in every state. In addition, they spent more money building new schools and improving existing ones than ever before. Traditional one-room rural schoolhouses were replaced by larger, more modern consolidated schools, which were centrally located so they could serve several communities.

School curriculum became more varied and interesting as educator John Dewey's theories were put into practice. Dewey believed that schools should do more than force children to learn mathematics and geography at the hand of a stern, ruler-wielding teacher. He suggested they should prepare students for life in a democratic society.

As a result, educators began concentrating on a child's complete intellectual development. Students still sat at desks and learned "reading, writing, and 'rithmetic," but they

Women and the Law

Despite women's greater independence in the 1920s, conservatism continued in the sphere of birth control and childbearing. The well-to-do generally enjoyed more options when it came to family planning and medical care, but ordinary women suffered, as this excerpt from Geoffrey Perrett's *America in the Twenties: A History* demonstrates.

"Thriving abortion clinics operated all over New York. They had become by the Twenties a rich source of payoff money for hundreds of policemen and politicians. When, as sometimes happened, a doctor was arrested for performing an illegal abortion it meant that he had forgotten or refused to pay up. In the country as a whole, it was estimated that up to 1 million women a year were criminally aborted. There was abortion by knitting needle, coat hanger, and buttonhook. Desperate women swallowed poisonous concoctions in an attempt to induce a miscarriage. Criminal abortion killed as many as 50,000 women a year. Yet it was absolutely against the law to disseminate birth control information or devices, under Section 211 of the United States Penal Code."

also studied music, art, home economics, and bookkeeping. After class, they took part in activities such as student government, dances, pep clubs, and sports. "When I graduated early in the [1890s] there weren't many boys—only two in our class and a dozen girls," said one father. "All our studies seemed very far away from real life, but today—they've got shop and athletics, and it's all nearer what a boy's interested in."[56]

Loss of Control

As school began to play a larger role in young people's lives, parents noticed that family life was changing. Sons and daughters went out in the evenings, even on school nights, for club meetings and sports events. Dances, parties, and church outings lasted until close to midnight. Teachers testified that late-night activities often caused poor classroom performance. "Now they all belong to two or three clubs and come to me morning after morning, heavy eyed, with work not done, and tell of being up until twelve or one the night before,"[57] one teacher observed.

Parents also discovered that children became more expensive as their social lives blossomed. Club dues, gas for the car, and dates took money. Clothing was more expensive, too, and young people were especially concerned about wearing the latest fashions. Girls who wanted to fit in scorned cotton dresses and cotton stockings in favor of silk. One woman remarked, "The dresses girls wear to school now used to be considered party dresses. My daughter would consider herself terribly abused if she had to wear the same dress to school two successive days."[58] Stylish young men preferred, in the words of one menswear salesman, "nifty suits that look like those everyone else buys and like they see

in the movies,"[59] rather than inexpensive jackets and trousers. Some teens even dropped out of school because they did not have proper clothing.

Sheiks and Shebas

Despite such seemingly trivial concerns, high school attendance more than doubled in the twenties. Enrollment in colleges increased dramatically as well. "We never thought of going to college," the wife of a businessman observed. "Our children never thought of anything else."[60]

Students recognized that they needed specialized training if they were going to succeed in the workplace, and they often chose to take classes in practical majors such as engineering, management, and economics. Classes, however, often took a backseat to social activities. Sororities and fraternities were popular on most campuses. So were football games, parties, and dances. "If you were a college fellow and you were on the right lists, you went to these debutante parties where the liquor would flow and maybe two big orchestras would play," remembered one young man from Maryland. "It was a very exciting period, because all you needed was a tuxedo and tails and you could go out every night."[61]

College men and women—known as "sheiks" and "shebas" after Rudolph Valentino's hit movie *The Sheik*—often had a reputation for wildness and irresponsibility. Thousands skipped class, drank too much, tore around the country in their cars, and worried their parents. "They're all desperadoes, these kids, all of them with any life in their veins; the girls as well as the boys; maybe more than the boys,"[62] wrote author Warner Fabian in his 1923 novel *Flaming Youth*. Undoubtedly, there were many sensible young men and women

Educational opportunities for all children increased as school attendance was made mandatory in every state by the end of the decade.

who quietly got an education and graduated. They were the overlooked minority, however.

Flapper Jane

Whether they were in college or on the job, modern young women of the twenties were known as "flappers," so called because of their habit of wearing unbuckled galoshes that flapped when they walked. Whereas females of earlier decades had worn long skirts, long hair, heavy cotton underwear, heavy black stockings, and ankle-binding shoes, flappers had bobbed hair (chin-length or shorter) and sometimes went to a beauty parlor and got it styled into a marcel—an arrangement of soft waves. They wore short dresses, sheer silk stockings, and heavy makeup, and did not own a corset, bra, or pet-

ticoat. One author described a fictitious "flapper Jane": "Jane isn't wearing much this summer. If you'd like to know exactly, it is: one dress, one step-in [undergarment], two stockings, two shoes."[63]

The contrast between the flapper's moral code and that of young women of the past was sharp as well. Unmarried girls in earlier decades were expected to be innocent, pure, and ignorant of anything having to do with sex. After marriage, they were to be devoted to their husbands and children. One author explained, "Young girls must look forward in innocence . . . to a romantic love match which would lead them to the altar and to living happily-ever-after; and until the 'right man' came along they must allow no male to kiss them."[64]

In contrast, flappers were characterized by a carefree, worldly, and independent spirit.

A young flapper stands next to her roadster. Young people often owned cars and had the reputation for speeding and driving drunk.

They delighted in shocking their elders, not only by their flimsy dresses and scarlet lips but also by their rudeness and vulgarity. Flappers chewed gum, told dirty jokes, and used profanity and slang such as "baloney" (nonsense), "cat's meow" (wonderful), and "cake-eater" (a ladies' man). They got drunk often and stayed out late at night with modern young men who dressed in "Oxford bags" (wide-leg trousers) and raccoon coats and had their hair parted in the middle and slicked down with Vaseline or brilliantine.

Most flappers and their boyfriends had cars and drove them fast. Accidents were common because of their habit of drinking and driving. Cars were also convenient places where couples could "neck," "pet," and have sex. A mother commented, "In 1890 a 'well-brought-up' boy and girl were commonly forbidden to sit together in the dark. . . . In an auto, however, a party may go to a city halfway across the state in an afternoon or evening, and unchaperoned automobile parties as late as midnight, while subject to criticism, are not exceptional."[65] One juvenile court judge condemned the car as a house of prostitution on wheels.

The Moral Gown

Not surprisingly, many conservative Americans preferred the earlier customs and opposed the shocking manners of the younger generation. "Girls are far more aggressive today. They call the boys up to try to make dates with them as they never would have when I was a girl,"[66] said one midwestern mother.

Some people took steps to stop the trend, starting with women's clothing. They created standards for a "moral gown," an ankle-length dress with a high neckline and long sleeves made of cotton, wool, or any other sturdy material. Authorities in some states even tried to legislate a dress code. In Utah, legislators passed a law that skirts be no higher than three inches off the ground. In Philadelphia, the "see level" was seven and a half inches. Other cities and states set their own standards for hems and necklines. While some conservative women conformed to these standards, most younger women ignored them, as a 1921 article in the *New Republic* illustrates: "At noon the girl workers hurry along the stone-walled canyons, gay as a crocus bed in spring sunshine. . . . Not one in ten is wearing the modest and durable frock recently recommended by . . . clergymen."[67]

As older women saw how practical and comfortable short hair, short skirts, and lighter fabrics could be, many decided that they would follow their daughters' leads. Some shortened their skirts, and many cut their hair. One observer stated, "In the latter years

The Decade of Bad Manners

In *Only Yesterday: An Informal History of the 1920's*, Frederick Lewis Allen describes the revolt against accepted manners and morals that characterized the post–World War I years. The revolt was expressed in many ways, but the decline in manners was a particularly difficult problem for society-minded hostesses to deal with, as the following excerpt illustrates.

"Manners became not merely different, but—for a few years—unmannerly. It was no mere coincidence that during this decade hostesses . . . found that their guests couldn't be bothered to speak to them on arrival or departure; that 'gatecrashing' at dances became an accepted practice; that thousands of men and women made a point of not getting to dinners within half an hour of the appointed time lest they seem insufficiently *blasé*; that house parties of flappers and their wide-trousered swains [boyfriends] left burning cigarettes on the mahogany tables, scattered ashes light-heartedly on the rugs, took the porch cushions out in the boats and left them there to be rained on, without apology; or that men and women . . . absorbed a few cocktails and straightaway turned a dinner party into a boisterous rout. . . . The old bars were down, no new ones had been built, and meanwhile the pigs were in the pasture. Some day, perhaps, the ten years which followed the war may aptly be known as the Decade of Bad Manners."

A group of flappers enjoy a cigarette on the beach. Millions of women took up smoking in the twenties.

of the decade bobbed hair became almost universal among girls in their twenties, very common among women in their thirties and forties, and by no means rare among women of sixty."[68]

Older women also joined the younger women in taking up cigarette smoking. In the early 1920s, only a few women smoked cigarettes, but within a few years, millions smoked. According to one historian, "[They] strewed the dinner table with their ashes, snatched a puff between the acts [of plays], invaded the masculine sanctity of the club car [on the train], and forced department stores

to place ornamental ash-trays between the chairs in their women's shoe departments."[69] President Coolidge's wife, Grace, was not to be left out of the new trend. She was the first First Lady to smoke in the White House.

The Lost Generation

On the surface, young people appeared to live solely for fun in the twenties, but many were, in fact, disillusioned with life. World War I with all its suffering and dying had not yielded world peace. Trouble continued to fester in postwar Germany and Communist-led Russia. American society seemed shallower than ever before, lacking in vision or idealism, obsessed with material things, hypocritical, and dehumanizing. "The older generation had certainly pretty well ruined this world before passing it on to us. They give us this Thing, knocked to pieces, leaky, red-hot, threatening to blow up; and then they are surprised that we don't accept it with the same enthusiasm with which they received it,"[70] said one young man.

Some of the most disenchanted were young intellectuals and artists, including Ernest Hemingway, F. Scott Fitzgerald, William Carlos Williams, Thornton Wilder, Archibald MacLeish, and Hart Crane. One of their contemporaries, author Gertrude Stein, nicknamed them the "Lost Generation." In their conversation, their writing, and their art, this group criticized and "debunked" (discredited) everything that Americans valued most. They ridiculed religion, politics, democracy, and middle-class life in general. Nobel Prize–winner Sinclair Lewis's books are some of the best examples of their philosophy. His novel *Babbitt* is the story of a small-town American businessman who blindly conforms to the standards and ethics of his world, and *Main Street* emphasizes the monotony and frustration of life in a small midwestern town. F. Scott Fitzgerald also mocked the American dream in his books *The Great Gatsby* and *Tender Is the Night.*

Many members of the Lost Generation so scorned U.S. society that they chose to go overseas and live as exiles in Paris. There, they devoted themselves to their art and to the pursuit of pleasure, which usually involved drinking, taking drugs, indulging in casual sex, and throwing wild parties. One young man wrote, "The greatest problems of the world . . . do not concern me in the slightest. What concerns me alone is myself and the interests of a few close friends."[71] Despite the fact that they were doing what they wanted to do, the group remained restless and unhappy, searching unsuccessfully for meaning in their lives.

Worthy of Being Idolized

While the Lost Generation ridiculed middle-class America, middle-class Americans had mixed feelings about intellectuals and artists. On one hand, they were seen as spoiled, out of touch, and overly critical. On the other, they were attractive, confident, and famous, and thus worthy of being idolized. According to one author, "Writers (and painters and musicians) were scorned, yet if successful—that is, if they made news or made money—they were admired extravagantly as people who had somehow gotten away with something."[72]

Hero worship—even of those who did not deserve acclaim—was strong in the '20s. Americans became excited over anyone and anything that was glamorous, notorious, or out of the ordinary. One observer pointed out, "Each new day saw some new development reported on the front page of the papers. Anyone who could do anything longer or harder or faster than anyone else was a champion, and it didn't matter of what."[73] The time was unparalleled for its crazy and extravagant exploits. Its wealth of wonderful nonsense— from cross country marathons to crossword puzzle addictions—made it the most zany decade of the twentieth century.

Wonderful Nonsense

As with any decade, the 1920s had its share of problems—youthful rebellion, inner-city poverty, illegal drinking, and a rise in organized crime, to name a few. Many Americans did not want to think about those problems, however. In fact, millions preferred to distract themselves by enjoying more fun, fads, and heroic exploits than in any previous age. As one '20s journalist wrote, "The right to play is the final clause in the charter of democracy. The people are king—*et le roi s'amuse* [and the king has fun]."[74]

Radio

Radio was the premier entertainment of the age, the activity that almost everyone was able to enjoy. Before 1920, radios were crystal sets used primarily by a few hobbyists in their experimental laboratories. In the fall of 1920, however, the first radio station, KDKA in Pittsburgh, came on the air. By September, there were three more stations, and by the end of the year, more than twenty-five. Most of them were small, and programming was extremely limited, usually a station announcement, a weather report, and some music. Still, those families who had radios loved to listen to them, even though they had to cluster closely around their sets to decipher the scratchy reception.

Soon, radios went on sale in stores. They were ugly boxes with dials, a horn loudspeaker, and an outside antenna one hundred feet long, and they required two sets of bat-

teries that had to be changed often. Nevertheless, they were affordable enough to be irresistible. "We spent close to $100 on our radio, and we built it ourselves at that," said one woman. "Where'd we get the money? Oh, out of our savings, like everybody else."[75] Stores sold out of radios almost as quickly as they came in stock. Neighborhoods sprouted forests of rooftop antennas. Revenue from the sales of radios totaled $11 million in 1922 and more than doubled that in 1923.

By 1926, the radio had developed from a simple box into an elaborate piece of furniture that was the centerpiece of the living room. Programming, too, improved, especially after advertisers realized that radio was a perfect way to get exposure for their products. Families enjoyed shows like *The Chase and Sanborn* (coffee) *Hour, The Eveready* (battery) *Hour*, and *The Smith Brothers* (cough drops) *Show*. Soon there was something for everyone. *The Fred Waring Show* featured music. *The Smith Family* was one of radio's first sitcoms. *Uncle Don's* was a children's variety show.

In 1928, *Amos 'n' Andy*, a fifteen-minute comedy show based on the lives of two black men, came on the air and soon became a favorite. The show's stars delighted millions of listeners with comic lines such as "I'se regusted" and "Holy mackerel, Andy!"[76] Although much of the material was based on racial stereotypes and would be offensive today, the show was so popular that Americans scheduled their evenings around its seven o'clock broadcast.

Stores and theaters sometimes aired the program to keep patrons from rushing home, and even President Calvin Coolidge reportedly demanded that he be undisturbed during the fifteen minutes it was on. "Radio was to the air as the automobile was to the earth, an agent of transport to a world as wide open as the imagination,"[77] said one observer.

The "Tabs"

Radio was very popular, but people still enjoyed reading as well. In addition to books and newspapers, there were new periodicals—*Reader's Digest*, established in 1922, and *Time* magazine, established in 1923—which summarized the news in a lively way. There was also H.L. Mencken's *American Mercury* (started in 1924), which was highly popular with intellectuals who appreciated the magazine's attacks on hypocrisy and pretense.

Some of the most garish publications in the '20s were the tabloids. The "tabs," as they were nicknamed, included the New York *Daily News*, established in 1919; the New York *Daily Mirror*, started in 1924; and the *Evening Graphic*, started shortly thereafter

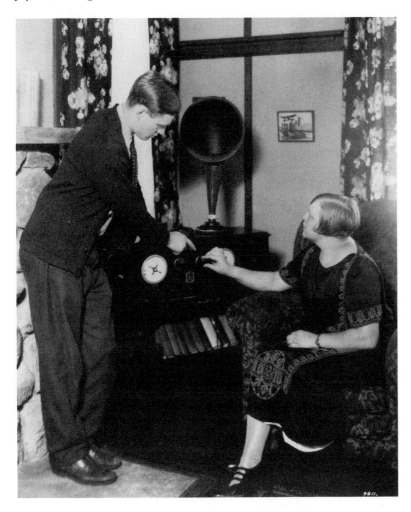

Radio was the most popular form of entertainment in the twenties, with families often huddling around their sets to listen to their favorite radio programs.

The discovery of the bullet-riddled body of Hollywood director William Desmond Taylor in February 1922 was guaranteed to boost sales of the tabloids. The following article from the New York *Daily News*, reprinted in Ezra Bowen's *This Fabulous Century*, played up every detail of the murder mystery. Despite an assortment of tantalizing clues, the case was never solved.

"All Hollywood is being raked for the killer of William Desmond Taylor; all the queer meeting places of the actors and actresses, directors and assistant directors, cameramen and extras—restaurants, beauty parlors, studios, dens where opium and marihuana and other strange drugs are common, dens where men and women dress in silk kimonos and sit in circles and drink odd drinks—are being visited.

Every one who has come into contact with the slain director, no matter how remotely, is being questioned. Things that may shock the world of moving picture fans are destined to come out of the mystery, it is said. Popular stars, male and female, may be scorched and smirched before the police investigation is over. And all the sins of the cinema colony will be made known. Dope fiends will figure in the tale before it is all told, and strange effeminate men and peculiarly masculine women.

The police are working now on two theories. One is that a beautiful woman is in the back of the affair—some one of the hundreds of beautiful women of the studio world. Perhaps she was a woman scorned or the sweetheart of another man, perhaps—but there are many motives and the police have not yet decided on any.

The other theory involves an enemy, made in the mysterious past of the dead man which he so well kept from his friends in Hollywood. Detectives piecing together the mosaic of Taylor's life came today upon some colored fragments that do not seem to fit and there are other fragments that are missing."

and quickly nicknamed the "Pornographic." The tabs specialized in the sensational and the dramatic. The latest society and Hollywood news, scandals, and gossip were included within their pages, and they introduced terms such as "love nest" (an apartment or other refuge for lovers), "sugar daddy" (a wealthy man who gives gifts to a young woman in exchange for sexual favors or companionship), and "torch murder" (murder for love) into the American vocabulary. Pictures and stories in tabloids were often faked, but there were plenty of authentic features. The most grisly photo of the decade, a 1928 snap-shot of condemned murderer Ruth Snyder strapped in the electric chair, appeared on the front page of a tab.

One of the most scandalous tabloid articles was the sex saga of "Daddy and Peaches," fifty-two-year-old millionaire Edward West Browning and fifteen-year-old schoolgirl Frances Heenan. The two were married in 1926, and after six months of marriage, Heenan sued Browning for divorce. During the trial, she claimed that Browning had caused her mental anguish by his practical jokes and sexually perverse behavior. "My happiness, my future, everything I had, was sacrificed on the altar of his selfishness,"[78] Peaches testified. The public devoured every detail of their bizarre relationship, but they had no say in the outcome of the trial. Browning won the case after the judge ruled that Heenan's testimony was not credible.

Confession magazines, similar to the tabloids, were also popular because of their emphasis on sex. Stories with titles such as "What I Told My Daughter the Night Before Her Marriage" and "The Confessions of a Chorus Girl" were guaranteed to attract readers, even though most were undoubtedly disappointed by the mildness of the articles. One newsman who toured the country in 1925 nevertheless remarked that "between

Millionaire Edward West Browning takes a stroll with his young wife, Peaches.

the magazines and the movies a lot of these little towns seem literally saturated with sex."[79]

"Let Yourself Go"

Americans who were attracted to sex in the tabloids found it even more irresistible at the movies. Sexual references were subtle compared to today's explicitness, but they were shocking enough to attract plenty of viewers. Movies had titles such as *Sinners in Silk* and *Virgin Paradise*, and trailers promised "Brilliant men, beautiful jazz babies, champagne baths, midnight revels, petting parties in the purple dawn, all ending in one terrific smashing climax that makes you gasp."[80]

Not all movies were about sex and seduction. Actor Tom Mix made the Western popular. Charlie Chaplin, Buster Keaton, and Harold Lloyd delighted viewers with their comedic shenanigans. In 1927, audiences enjoyed the first motion picture with sound, *The Jazz Singer*, the story of an aspiring Broadway singer whose father wanted him to continue the family tradition of being a cantor in a synagogue. In 1928, Walt Disney introduced Mickey Mouse in the cartoon "Plane Crazy," beginning an era of animation. "Go to a motion picture . . . and let yourself go," encouraged the *Saturday Evening Post*. "All the adventure, all the romance, all the excitement you lack in your daily life are in—Pictures. They take you completely out of yourself into a wonderful new world."[81]

Americans took the advice. By the end of the decade, 100 million men, women, and children—almost the entire population of the United States—went to a movie every week. Movies were a chance to get a glimpse of much-admired screen idols—gorgeous and mysterious

Greta Garbo, glamorous Joan Crawford, and brooding Ronald Coleman. Every detail of movie stars' lives seemed fascinating, from Mary Pickford's divorce and subsequent marriage to handsome Douglas Fairbanks to comedian Fatty Arbuckle's involvement in the death of actress Virginia Rappe. Millions of American women mourned the death of sex symbol Rudolph Valentino after he suffered a perforated ulcer and peritonitis in 1926. The *New York World* reported, "Fighting for a glimpse of Rudolph Valentino's body, 15,000 men and women stormed the Campbell Building at No. 1970 Broadway yesterday, precipitating a riot which assumed threatening proportions."[82]

Even for those who were not infatuated with a favorite star, movies were educational, giving people in small towns a fair portrayal of how the rest of the world lived, how they dressed, and how they passed their time. One woman wrote, "[From movies] we learned how tennis was played and golf, what a swimming pool was . . . and of course we learned about Love, a very foreign country like maybe China or Connecticut."[83]

Movies also provided a chance to enjoy the elegant atmosphere of the theater itself. In big cities and small towns, "dream palaces" featured large auditoriums decorated with marble pillars, velvet draperies, fine-art reproductions, and crystal chandeliers. One magazine writer said,

[The theatergoer's] feet sink in soft rugs, she is surrounded by heavy Renaissance tables, oil paintings, and statues of nudes. When she goes home that evening she will perhaps clean spinach and peel onions but for a few hours . . . she bathes in elegance and dignity; she satisfies her yearning for a cultural atmosphere. . . . In the de luxe house every man is a king and every woman a queen.[84]

A huge crowd gathers outside a movie theater in 1927 to see The Jazz Singer, *the first motion picture with sound.*

Will and "Lucky Lindy"

There were other heroes in the twenties besides those who moved across theater screens. The public fell in love with comedian Will Rogers (who, in fact, starred in several movies) for his homespun humor, down-to-earth philosophy, and generous spirit. Millions read his column, which appeared in more than 350 daily newspapers. It contained such wry comments as "Things in our country run in spite of government. Not by aid of it," and "If all politicians fished instead of spoke

publicly, we would be at peace with the world."[85]

Explorer Richard E. Byrd was another popular figure of the time. Millions of Americans followed his exploits as he made his journey to Antarctica in 1929. Byrd radioed the *New York Times* the moment he became the first person to fly over the South Pole. When he returned, he was given a New York ticker-tape parade. The festivities were broadcast by radio across the country. "The most extensive and far-reaching radio network ever assembled to carry the description of a returning hero . . . functioned perfectly yesterday to tell the story of how Rear Admiral Byrd and his comrades came up the harbor and were received at City Hall after sixteen months in the Antarctic,"[86] the *New York Times* proclaimed.

Despite the nation's admiration for Byrd and his accomplishments, the foremost hero of the decade was Charles Lindbergh, a tall, slender, twenty-four-year-old pilot who was the first person to make a nonstop solo flight across the Atlantic. In a time of flamboyance and declining morals, Lindbergh was modest, ethical, and upright. He did not smoke or drink and worked hard to live up to the high standards of diligence, enterprise, honesty, and unselfishness that he set for himself.

On May 27, 1927, Lindbergh took off on his record-setting flight from Roosevelt Field, New York, in a single-engine monoplane called the *Spirit of St. Louis*. For the next thirty-three hours and thirty-two minutes, everyone waited breathlessly to see if he would make it to Paris. When the news came that he had safely landed there, the entire nation exploded with happiness. On his triumphant arrival home, an estimated 4.5 million New Yorkers turned out to greet him. One American wrote,

People crowd in around the Spirit of St. Louis *to congratulate the plane's pilot, Charles Lindbergh, the first person to make a nonstop solo flight across the Atlantic.*

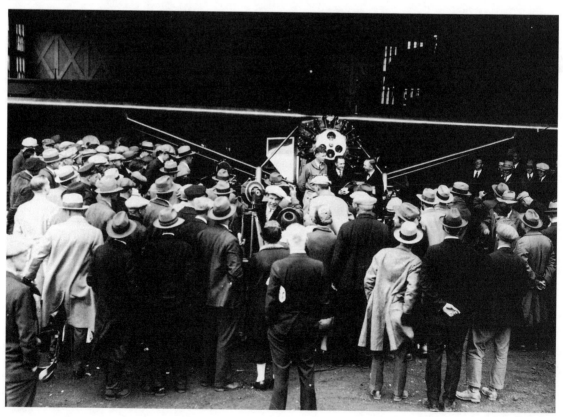

We shouted ourselves hoarse. Not because a man had flown across the Atlantic! Not even because he was an American! But because he was as clean in character as he was strong and fine in body; because he put "ethics" above any desire for wealth; because he was as modest as he was courageous; and because—as we now know, beyond any shadow of doubt—*these are the things which we honor most* in life. To have shown us this truth about ourselves is the biggest thing that Lindbergh has done.[87]

Lindbergh reflected the good in America, and the country's interest in flight. Many people were tempted to try flying themselves. There was also a sharp increase in passenger flights after Lindy's 1927 triumph. In an effort to increase the public's interest in airplanes as well as make money, pilots who had flown during the war showcased their flying skills by "barnstorming" (so called because planes were parked in barns at night). They would fly about the country, attracting an audience by performing stunts such as acrobatics and wing walking, and then offer members of the crowd five-minute joy rides for $5. There were always a few courageous souls who dared to soar above their admiring friends, especially after they were reassured by the pilot: "All rides are guaranteed to get you back in one piece. Your money back if you get killed."[88]

Johnny, Red, and the "Babe"

Even with Byrd, Lindbergh, and all the other amusements and distractions, Americans had plenty of time and energy to go crazy over sports during the 1920s. It did not matter if the activity was baseball, football, swimming, tennis, or golf. Fans participated and followed champion athletes with excitement and devotion.

There were many great athletes to be excited about. Nineteen-year-old Gertrude Ederle swam the English Channel in 1926. Olympic champion Johnny Weissmuller set sixty-seven swimming world records and went on to become a film star in Tarzan movies. Red Grange, the "Galloping Ghost," was named a three-time All-American and attracted large crowds who wanted to see him play football. Syndicated columnist Damon Runyon described Grange: "He is crashing sound. He is poetry. He is brute force. He is the doggonedest football player that the East has seen in many years, and you can say that again."[89]

Other athletes were just as notable. Golfer Bobby Jones gained renown for his thirteen national championships between 1921 and 1930. Prizefighters Jack Dempsey and Gene Tunney engaged in the "Battle of the Ages" in 1927 while a crowd of more than 100,000 watched the fight and 50 million listened to the radio broadcast of the contest. "Jack Dempsey was a great fighter—possibly the greatest that ever entered a ring,"[90] attested Tunney, who managed to beat Dempsey and retired undefeated from his heavyweight championship in 1928.

The sports darling of the decade was undoubtedly George Herman "Babe" Ruth. Unlike Lindbergh who was adored because he symbolized all that was good in America, Ruth was the "bad boy" of baseball. He smoked, drank, swore, chased women, and had no manners. He had a bad temper that he did not choose to control. Yet he was also full of raw exuberance, and he transformed the game of baseball, hitting a record sixty home runs in 1927. (When he retired in 1935, his career total of 714 home runs set a major

Despite Babe Ruth's personal flaws, people loved him for his zest for life, his dramatic rise from humble beginnings, and his love of baseball. Author Geoffrey Perrett gives further details about Ruth's charm in *America in the Twenties: A History*.

"[Babe Ruth] was one of the ugliest men ever to play the game, and one of the most lovable. He had a barrel torso, spindly legs, a strangely mincing pit-a-pat gait, an enormous head with tiny eyes, a squashed nose, and thick lips. Abandoned by his parents, he had grown up in a tough, shadowy world, without education, without love, and without illusions. He had known hunger. When he began to make a lot of money he became, and remained, a glutton. His pregame diet consisted of several hot dogs and a glass of water fizzing with bicarbonate of soda to help them on their way. . . .

Fame and riches did not change him one bit. In some respects he would never grow up. Yet the youthful characteristics he carried into adult life—the earnestness, the sense of fun, the importance he attached to friendship, the complete lack of pretension—these made him a man whom other men found easy to love. Alive with animal vitality, he raced around New York in a monogrammed roadster, bundled up in a raccoon coat, a huge cigar clamped between his teeth, as if determined to collect a speeding ticket a day. He radiated goodwill and sincerity. His delight in being 'the Babe' was almost childlike. Wherever he was, he remained completely himself."

Babe Ruth was the most beloved and idolized sports figure of the twenties.

league record that stood until 1974.) Known to his fans as the "Bambino" and the "Sultan of Swat," Ruth gave everyone what they wanted to see—balls belted out of the park, runners sliding into home plate, and triumphant victories. His presence and the excitement he generated drew more people to his games than at any other time in history. Harry Hooper, a Boston teammate of Ruth's, remembered, "[Babe was] the idol of American youth and the symbol of baseball the world over—a man loved by more people and with an intensity of feeling that perhaps has never been equaled before or since."[91]

Game Craze

Not every American could go see Babe Ruth or attend a ticker-tape parade, but almost everyone could—and did—enjoy simple pleasures such as playing games in the privacy of their homes. Bridge was the standard for social evenings among the upper middle class and well-to-do. A card game known as pedro (peedro) was played by the lower classes.

People also enjoyed playing checkers, backgammon, and dominoes.

In 1922, mah-jongg became a craze across the country. The game, imported from China, can best be described as a combination of dice and dominoes. It required 144 tiles and involved learning the meaning of terms such as "Pung," "Chow," "bamboos," "flowers," "South Wind," and "Red Dragon." Its rules and system of scoring were extremely complex, especially because a variety of confusing and contradictory rule books were available. As the *New York Times* explained in 1924, "Teachers [of mah-jongg] with social

New York society women play a game of mah-jongg, which became a national craze in 1922.

backing sprang up over night. . . . Each of these teachers, whether in New York or Washington or San Francisco society, promptly began teaching her own private method—one she might have 'developed' the night before."[92] Many people became so involved with mah-jongg that they purchased Chinese robes and Oriental tables in order to be truly authentic when they played. In 1922–1923, no dinner party was considered complete unless it ended with a few brisk rounds of play.

When the popularity of mah-jongg died down a little, many Americans became obsessed with crossword puzzles. Crossword puzzles had existed since about 1913, but in 1924 the new publishing firm Simon and Schuster produced the first book—complete with pencil attached—devoted solely to crossword puzzles. Hundreds of thousands of copies were sold, and other publishers rushed to print their own volumes. Sales of dictionaries and *Roget's Thesaurus* skyrocketed. At least one company created a wristband dictionary for those who wanted to work continuously at their puzzle solving.

There were a surprising number of people in that category. Newspapers carried stories of individuals like Mary Zaba, a "crossword widow" whose husband was so busy doing puzzles that he had no time to support his family. A New York man was arrested because he refused to leave a restaurant where he had spent four hours trying to finish a puzzle. The Baltimore and Ohio Railroad placed dictionaries on all its trains on the main line, and a traveler between New York and Boston claimed that about 60 percent of his fellow passengers did crosswords as they traveled. Any passerby on the street was liable to know standard crossword questions and answers such as "the name of the Egyptian sun god" (Ra or Re) and "a two-letter word for a printer's measure" (em).

Marathon Lunacy

For Americans who yearned for entertainment more exciting than going to the movies or doing crossword puzzles, various competitions were considered "the berries" (wonderful). In rocking chair derbies, pea-eating contests, and long-distance dance marathons, people vied for records, prizes, and fame. Their ingenuity at coming up with bizarre challenges prompted the *Saturday Evening Post* to observe that America was "first in war, first in peace, first in tree sitting, gum chewing, peanut pushing and bobbing up and down in water."[93]

Dance contests were some of the least bizarre competitions, since they stemmed from young people's love of dancing. Many modern couples liked to drive to dance halls, where entrance fees ranged from 50 cents to $1.50 for an evening of fun. To maintain decorum, some dance halls were overseen by female chaperones who made sure that acceptable moral conduct was maintained. For instance, partners were not allowed to dance with their cheeks touching—"it is simply a case of public lovemaking,"[94] stated one enforcer—and men were expected to keep their hand lightly on their partner's spine, above the waistline.

Dances such as the foxtrot, the shimmy, the toddle, and the Black Bottom, however, regularly violated the rules of behavior, and conservative Americans were horrified. "The embracing of partners—the female only half dressed—is absolutely indecent," stated the *Catholic Telegraph*. "The motions—they are such as may not be described, with any respect for propriety, in a family newspaper."[95]

Dance marathons, in which contestants competed to see who could stay on their feet the longest, were a grueling form of dance contest. As spectators cheered their favorites, participants danced until they were exhausted.

Contestants compete in a Coney Island dance marathon in 1928.

After hours and days, most could only prop each other up and sway back and forth. Some partners punched or kicked each other to stay awake. Nurses stood by on the sidelines to resuscitate dancers during periodic fifteen-minute breaks or when they collapsed. A few contestants died of heart failure. Marathons could last for a week or more; one Chicago contest dragged on for 119 days. "Of all the crazy competitions ever invented, the dancing marathon wins by a considerable margin of lunacy,"[96] stated the New York *World* in 1923.

The Bunion Derby

Marathon running was another punishing form of competition, and the longest mara-

thon of the '20s was the "Bunion Derby," a thirty-four-hundred-mile transcontinental race from Los Angeles to New York held in 1928 and 1929. Legendary sports promoter and showman C.C. "Cash and Carry" Pyle staged the event in the hopes that he would make millions in endorsements and entry fees.

Pyle did not have trouble finding entrants who were willing to test their speed and stamina. In 1928, almost 250 racers—the best in the world—entered the contest. By the end of the first day, however, 50 had dropped out, and the numbers continued to climb as exhaustion, blisters, and poor food took their toll.

The event was an enormous flop. Crowds that had been expected along the route did not show up. The run, which was supposed to take sixty-five days, took more than eighty. By the time the last runners limped into Madison Square Garden in New York City, few people were waiting to applaud them. First-place runner Andrew Payne was awarded $25,000, but Pyle ended up losing $100,000 that year.

The second year, the promoter was so broke that all the winners got for their efforts were sore feet and bad memories. "There has been a lot of talk about how much these boys suffered," Pyle said in one interview. "There is not one of them who suffered more than I did."[97]

Up a Pole

Perhaps the most unique fad of the decade began in 1924, when former boxer Alvin "Shipwreck" Kelly attracted nationwide attention by shimmying up a flagpole and perching there for over thirteen hours. Kelly's

sitting was a stunt for a Hollywood theater, but in the coming years he continued his peculiar occupation in a quest for fame and fortune. His efforts sparked hundreds of copycat sittings around the country.

The fad's popularity reached its peak in Baltimore, Maryland, in 1929 when in one week at least twenty pole-sitters made the news. Special attention was paid to fifteen-year-old Avon Foreman, who climbed up a sturdy hickory pole in his backyard in an effort to set the juvenile pole-sitting record. He was encouraged by five thousand neighbors and well-wishers, and remained aloft almost eleven days. The mayor of Baltimore sent Foreman a special letter to commemorate his success: "The grit and stamina evidenced by your endurance from July 20th to 30th, a period of 10 days, 10 hours, 10 minutes and 10 seconds atop of the 22 foot pole in the rear of your home shows that the old pioneer spirit of early America is being kept alive by the youth of today."[98]

Alvin "Shipwreck" Kelly sits perched atop a flagpole in 1929 in an attempt to set a new pole-sitting record.

A Revolt of the Emotions

Young white Americans in the twenties saw jazz as an exciting new sound and a forbidden pleasure. To blacks, however, jazz was part of their heritage, an expression of their joys and sorrows. In 1925, author J.A. Rogers attempted to define the sound and came to the conclusion that "jazz is rejuvenation, a recharging of the batteries of civilization with primitive new vigor." A portion of his article is included in *The Twenties: Fords, Flappers, and Fanatics*, edited by George E. Mowry.

"Jazz isn't music merely, it is a spirit that can express itself in almost anything. The true spirit of jazz is a joyous revolt from convention, custom, authority, boredom, even sorrow—from everything that would confine the soul of man and hinder its riding free on the air. The Negroes who invented it called their songs the 'Blues,' and they weren't capable of satire or deception. Jazz was their explosive attempt to cast off the blues and be happy, carefree happy even in the midst of sordidness and sorrow. And that is why it has been such a balm for modern ennui [boredom], and has become a safety valve for modern machine-ridden and convention-bound society. It is the revolt of the emotions against repression."

Jazz legend Louis Armstrong.

"Just Start Playing"

As Americans amused themselves with frivolous games, fads, and contests, a new kind of music—jazz—was coming of age in black nightclubs around the country. Originating in New Orleans, jazz was characterized by a sense of energy and a melody that did not always follow the beat. Above all, jazz involved improvising. Great jazz players created melody and variations according to their mood and used written music only as a guide for what they felt like playing. For instance, when the new pianist for Joe "King" Oliver's Creole Jazz Band asked for copies of the music the band played, "They politely told me they didn't have any. I then asked what key would the first number be in. I must have been speaking another language because [Joe Oliver] said, 'When you hear two knocks, just start playing.'"[99]

In the beginning, jazz was enjoyed only by blacks, who had to restrict themselves to segregated dance halls and nightclubs. Talented artists such as Louis Armstrong, Duke Ellington, Earl "Fatha" Hines, Fats Waller, and Bessie Smith performed in obscurity for years. Then in 1921, New Yorkers discovered the black musical *Shuffle Along,* which opened at the 63rd Street Musical Hall. Eight other all-black musicals soon followed, and Broadway playgoers began patronizing nightclubs in black sections of town in order to hear more of the catchy new sound.

Ironically, some of the most popular spots like the Cotton Club in Harlem had an all-black show but did not admit black patrons. "The whites from downtown could see a show right in the middle of Harlem with the cream of the black entertainment . . . and not have to be bothered rubbing elbows with the people who actually lived in the community,"[100] observed one performer.

Hot Jazz

Jazz was "hot," but it was also judged scandalous by conservative Americans. Because of its roots, they considered jazz primitive, barbaric, and vulgar. "It is merely an irritation of the nerves of hearing, a sensual teasing of the strings of physical passion," said one jazz critic of the time. Another wrote, "Never in the history of our land have there been such immoral conditions among our young people, and . . . the blame is laid on jazz music and its evil influence on the young people of today."[101]

The adult disapproval influenced the rebellious younger generation to go crazy over jazz. They saw it as the music of outcasts. They loved its energy and its brassiness. In order to dance to it, they learned complicated new steps like those of the Charleston, a dance that first appeared in the black revue

Runnin' Wild, which opened on Broadway in 1923. Critics had predicted that no one but a professional could do the Charleston, with its flying feet, knocking knees, and crossing hands, but thousands of young flappers and their partners mastered it and romped to it in the years to come.

Serious mainstream composers soon realized that jazz was an impressive new art form and began creating jazz melodies of their own. One of the best known was George Gershwin, whose jazz concerto *Rhapsody in Blue* premiered in 1924. "Men and women were fighting to get in the door," one man remembered

A couple demonstrates the Charleston, a complicated dance that became popular among flappers.

of opening night, "pulling and mauling each other as they sometimes do at a baseball game, or a prize fight, or in the subway."[102]

Taking advantage of the public's new focus on the black artistic community, black playwrights, classical musicians, historians, and artists were able to gain a broader audience for their work. Academic Alain Locke, writers Zora Neale Hurston and Claude McKay, poet Langston Hughes, and others challenged the nation to think about the black American experience. A poem by Hughes is one illustration of their efforts:

My folks and my folks' folkses/And their folkses before

Have been here 300 years or more—

Yet any foreigner from Polish to Dutch/Rides anywhere he wants to

And is not subject to such

Treatments as my fellow-men give me/In this Land of the Free.[103]

Discrimination against African Americans was only one of the troubling aspects of life during the Roaring Twenties. Prohibition—the federal ban on alcohol—was another expression of misguided thinking that many Americans defended and supported. What came out of Prohibition—invasions of privacy, the escalation of organized crime, and the rise of men like Al Capone—spelled danger to innocent individuals and threatened the order and security of American society as well.

"Goodbye, John Barleycorn"

The Eighteenth Amendment to the Constitution prohibited the manufacture, sale, transportation, and import of intoxicating liquors in the United States. It did not meet much organized opposition when Congress passed it in late 1917. The country was involved in World War I, and Americans were highly idealistic. They were helping to save the world and make it safe for democracy. The notion of improving their own society by outlawing "demon rum" and other alcoholic beverages seemed right and proper.

By January 1919, the necessary three-fourths of the states had ratified the amendment. Congress passed the Volstead Act in October 1919, defining intoxicating liquors, providing for agents to enforce the law, and setting penalties for its violation. "The Noble Experiment," as President Herbert Hoover would call it, went into effect at midnight on January 16, 1920, with apparent national support. "Goodbye, John Barleycorn. You were God's worst enemy. You were Hell's best friend. The reign of tears is over,"[104] proclaimed evangelist Billy Sunday.

The "Dry" Movement

The thinking that prompted a nation of drinkers to go "dry" in 1920 seems foolish and impractical today. Saloons, taverns, and drinking had always been a part of American society. From the nation's beginnings, colonists drank beer, wine, rum, and hard cider, in part

because such drinks were often safer than impure water and unpasteurized milk. Many immigrants came from cultures where wine and beer were an integral part of life as well.

The problem of drunkenness, however, particularly the growing problem of a breadwinner drinking up the family's rent and grocery money, caused some people to view alcohol as a national curse. It impaired health, ruined character, and led people into crime. Opponents of drinking at first urged temperance—moderate consumption or voluntary abstinence. In time, however, their goal became the passage of a national prohibition law.

Millions of people eventually became convinced that alcohol and saloons were sinful and destructive. Prohibitionist groups such as the Women's Christian Temperance Union and the Anti-Saloon League won converts by addressing public meetings, organizing petitions, and lobbying Congress for their cause. They received support from churchgoers and conservatives, who also helped pass state and local prohibition laws. "My objection to the saloon-keeper is the same that I have to the louse," said one man. "He makes his living off the head of a family."[105]

"The Law Will Be Obeyed"

On the night that Prohibition went into effect, bells rang out and crowds gathered in churches across the land to greet the new, alcohol-free era. John F. Kramer, the first

Members of the Women's Christian Temperance Union campaign for Prohibition in 1917.

Prohibition commissioner, optimistically proclaimed,

> The law will be obeyed in cities, large and small, and in villages, and where it is not obeyed it will be enforced. . . . The law says that liquor to be used as a beverage must not be manufactured. We shall see that it is not manufactured. Nor sold, nor given away, nor hauled in anything on the surface of the earth or under the earth or in the air.[106]

But enforcing Prohibition was easier said than done. At first, most Americans respected the new law and had high hopes that it would reduce crime and other social ills. From the beginning, however, the nation was not entirely dry. Many people who had supported Prohibition in 1917 decided that they were not ready to stop drinking for the rest of their lives. Others had never supported passage of the amendment. Before Prohibition took effect, they had stockpiled large amounts of wine, beer, and hard liquor to drink in the privacy of their own homes. (Oddly, *drinking* alcohol was not prohibited under the Volstead Act.) Their neighbors who had not had such foresight began buying small one-gallon stills with which to make home brew. Many people also discovered that it was fairly easy to buy illegal liquor.

Over time, millions of otherwise law-abiding citizens became "scofflaws"—habitual or flagrant violators of Prohibition. Little old ladies sold beer. Children delivered liquor for their parents who manufactured it as a sideline to legitimate business. Some of the nation's most prominent leaders were "wet." New York mayor Jimmy Walker received weekly deliveries of booze. Congressman Fiorello LaGuardia demonstrated how to make beer at a press conference. Alice Roosevelt Longworth, the wife of the Speaker of the House of Representatives, admitted that she and her husband had a small still in their home. "If you think this country ain't dry, just watch 'em vote; if you think this country ain't wet, just watch 'em drink,"[107] quipped Will Rogers.

The Real McCoy

Although alcohol was banned in the United States, its manufacture was legal in neighboring countries. In northern states, smugglers crossed the border into Canada, made their purchases, and carried cases of liquor back into the United States under the cover of darkness. In Detroit, Michigan, boats were the most common vehicles used in smuggling liquor across the Detroit River, and when the river froze in the winter, people walked, sledded, and even drove cars packed with whiskey across the ice. Detroit became known as a "wide-open booze town" because of all the alcohol coming in from Canada. "The illegal liquor industry was one-eighth the size of the automobile industry and turned over more than $200 million every year,"[108] said one Detroit journalist.

Some smugglers went south to get liquor—especially rum—from Mexico and the Ba-

A congressman openly serves up alcoholic cider he made in his own backyard. Such flagrant violations of Prohibition among otherwise law-abiding citizens were common.

hamas. Coast Guard officials were always on the alert to arrest those bringing in liquor by boat, so rumrunners, as the smugglers were called, usually waited just outside U.S. territorial waters (three nautical miles off the coast, later changed to twelve nautical miles). Their line of boats, standing off New York and Boston harbor, came to be called Rum Row. Buyers in small, fast boats would dash out from shore (again, usually in the dead of night), take the alcohol aboard, and then dart back to some safe, hidden harbor.

One of the most famous rumrunners of the time was Bill McCoy, a boatbuilder from Jacksonville, Florida. McCoy realized that he could make a fortune bringing liquor into the United States, and he promptly purchased a schooner and began smuggling. "We transact business here day and night," McCoy told a man who visited his boat as it lay off the coast of Massachusetts. "We manage to supply Block Island, Martha's Vineyard, New Bedford, and Fall River with what the residents of those places seem to want the most. Come out any time you want to; the law can't touch us here, and we'll be very glad to see you."[109]

Because he tried to provide only the best liquor, McCoy's goods became known as "the real McCoy," a term that has persisted into modern times. Despite the risks of his trade, which included several run-ins with the Coast Guard and time spent in prison, McCoy eventually retired on his profits, which totaled over $1 million.

Buyer Beware

Since virtually everything having to do with alcohol was illegal during the twenties, making alcohol was unregulated during Prohibition. There were no production guidelines, no standards of quality, and no inspectors to en-sure that the alcohol a person drank was safe or "the real McCoy." Anyone who wanted to concoct an alcoholic beverage and sell it (illegally of course) did so. The motto of the country was "buyer beware" because most available alcohol was adulterated in some way.

Industrial alcohol—grain alcohol produced for use in the manufacture of rayon, antifreeze, shaving cream, photographic film, and so forth—accounted for much of the liquor consumed during Prohibition. Most industrial alcohol contained bad-tasting or poisonous substances such as soap, sulfuric acid, or wood alcohol that had been specifically added during production to prevent people from trying to drink it. Bootleggers—people who illegally manufactured, sold, or smuggled alcohol—found it relatively easy to remove the contaminants, however, by "cooking" or redistilling. They then mixed the pure alcohol with flavors and additives such as caramel coloring, prune juice, fusel oil (poisonous oil occurring in imperfectly distilled alcoholic products), or even a little good liquor to give it an authentic taste and appearance.

Glycerin and oil of juniper produced an approximation of gin known as "bathtub gin" (so called because the water used in making it was often drawn from a bathtub tap). Caramel, prune juice, and creosote made Scotch whiskey. While good liquor could take years to make and age, the hallmark of bootleg operations was speed. An observer pointed out, "Often in one night the denatured alcohol is redistilled, colored, flavored, bottled, labeled and shipped."[110]

White Lightning and Soda Pop Moon

Moonshine whiskey was a favorite of bootleggers and drinkers during Prohibition.

Moonshine had been made in the Appalachian Mountains since the 1700s and was traditionally prepared from grain (often corn), sugar, and water. During Prohibition, however, lawless brewers made their moonshine from less healthy products. Prohibition agents often found chunks of bone, decayed meat, carcasses of rats, cats, mice, or dead cockroaches in stills that they raided. "The more juicy the garbage, the better the mash, and the better the 'shine,'"[111] one man claimed.

Various types of moonshine went by names such as White Lightning (made from corn), Jackass Brandy (made from peaches and well known for causing internal bleeding), Yack Yack Bourbon (Chicago moonshine flavored with iodine and burnt sugar), and Soda Pop Moon (Philadelphia whiskey containing a heavy dose of isopropyl alcohol). Because making moonshine was inexpensive and easy, many people chose to make their own. A hundred pounds of sugar cost only $5, and small stills could be purchased in hardware stores for about $7. Grain, copper tubing, and kettles were readily available, and novice moonshiners could even find recipes and tips in their neighborhood libraries.

Two sisters stand guard over their family's moonshine business in St. Paul, Minnesota, during Prohibition.

Liquid Death

Americans found it hard to resist the profits to be made from bootlegging in the '20s. Some bootleggers were criminals, some were southern mountain men, but many were just ordinary people like Jennie Justo, a resident of Madison, Wisconsin. Justo put herself through college selling bootlegged wine (made by local Italians), and then went on to run a speakeasy for college students. She was caught and jailed for her illegal activities but continued to regard them as "a respectable way of making a living and of fulfilling a community need."[112]

Not all bootleggers were as harmless as Justo, especially those who were careless about removing poisons from their product. For instance, some operators did not discard the "heads" and "tails" (beginning and end) of a production run, which were contaminated by deadly aldehydes and fusel oil. Some still operators unwittingly used defective

The Smell of Bootleg Hooch

For some Americans, Prohibition meant bootleggers and speakeasies. For others, such as Frank Brookhouser who grew up in Ford City, Pennsylvania, it meant small-boy drama, cops-and-robber raids, and a powerful stench that lingered long after the excitement was over. Brookhouser's reminiscences are included in *These Were Our Years*.

"Whenever the police raided a still, it made for an exciting time and a god-awful smell in the neighborhood. They would bring the bootleg hooch—and the criminals, the law-breakers—to the police station and a crowd would quickly gather.

Every boy in the neighborhood who wasn't bedded down with pneumonia, small pox, whooping cough, mumps, measles, or some such thing would certainly be in the crowd, peeking into the police station, trying to get a glimpse of the bootleggers as they were put behind bars.

That was all right. That was drama.

But then the police would pour all of the hooch into the alley to get rid of it—and that wasn't so good. On a hot summer night—the raids always seemed to be made at evening time—the aroma of the stuff would permeate the area. And it lingered.

It was even there the next day when we went out into our back yards to play some more and talk about the excitement of the night before. So I can truthfully say that I was very familiar with bootleg hooch, even though I never tasted the stuff. It must have tasted awful, if it was anything like it smelled."

An official destroys barrels of bootleg alcohol during a police raid.

coils that allowed copper, lead, and zinc salts to pollute the moonshine. Others bottled their product in old-fashioned fruit jars with zinc lids that corroded and leached toxins into the drink.

Sometimes, bootleggers deliberately used toxic substances, such as sulfuric acid, creosote, or embalming fluid, to give their product more flavor and kick. Sadly, many customers were fooled. "Boy!" they would say. "This is good, strong stuff. Burns [the] hell out of my throat!"[113] Occasionally, the poor and ignorant poisoned themselves by drinking rubbing alcohol, wood alcohol, cheap hair tonic, and varnish mixtures because they could not afford bootleg whiskey. The results were tragic.

In 1928 in New York City, a batch of liquor containing wood alcohol killed twenty-five men in three days. In 1930, an estimated fifteen thousand people drank liquor containing the extract of Jamaican ginger (known as jake), a cheap ingredient that was almost 90 percent alcohol. The result was an epidemic of "jake paralysis," which one journalist of the time described: "The feet of the paralyzed ones drop forward from the ankle so that the toes point downward. . . . The calves of his legs, after two or three weeks, begin to soften and hang down; the muscles between thumbs and index fingers shrivel away."[114]

Treating "Thirstitis"

In addition to those who drank tainted alcohol and required medical attention, ordinary people turned to family doctors and pharmacists when suffering acute "thirstitis" during Prohibition. The law allowed doctors to prescribe alcohol, including wine, for medicinal purposes, but no patient could legally have more than a half-pint of alcohol every ten days. Many medicines such as cough syrups,

tonics and bracers, and heart cures had an alcohol base, too. Doctors were given a pad of one hundred blank prescription forms for medicinal liquor. These had to last ninety days and could be filled only by a pharmacist.

Doctors knew the pain and death that illegal alcohol caused. Many also believed that small amounts of whiskey, beer, and wine could have health benefits for their patients. Thus, in 1929 alone, they wrote over 10 million prescriptions for medicinal alcohol. Never had so many people been told to have a rum toddy for a sore throat, a glass of spiced wine for their digestive problems, or a shot of whiskey to steady their nerves.

Lollipops and Vine-Glo

Beer was the workingman's drink, so its loss was strongly felt in all parts of the country during Prohibition. Fortunately for beer drinkers, alcoholic beer was brewed in urban areas by gangsters who bought breweries from owners who had been put out of business by the ban. They then shipped their product around the country, making huge profits for themselves and delighting those who looked forward to having a drink after work.

Some breweries operated legally making "near beer"—beer with less than 1 percent alcohol content. Unfortunately, near beer was tasteless and had no kick. Bartenders were often willing to help out by spiking near beer with a shot of raw alcohol upon request. "Do you want a lollipop on the side with that?"[115] they would ask.

Many people made their own beer at home during Prohibition. Wort, a component of beer, could be purchased in stores along with the yeast that was used to complete the brewing process. Stores also carried several do-it-yourself products for those who wanted

Drinking was part of Italian, German, Polish, and Irish culture, and many immigrants who came from those countries quietly violated Prohibition by making wine or liquor so they could drink in the privacy of their own homes. Not every immigrant family went as far as John Morahan's, however. His story is included in Peter Jennings and Todd Brewster's *The Century*.

"My mother was Irish, from county Sligo, and for her making booze was a family tradition. In Ireland, everyone makes their own stuff. So when she got here to New York, she and my father bought some rooming houses, and when Prohibition hit, she just started making booze in the kitchen and selling it from the ground floor. She was a real businesswoman, my mother, and I guess I took after her. As a teenager, I was already driving around in a Nash convertible making deliveries and running four speakeasies. . . .

Our speakeasies were just like a regular bar you'd see today except for the door with the peephole in it. We had to be careful who we let in and we knew our customers on a first name basis—they were like family. If a stranger were to come in and he turned out to be a government agent and you sold him anything, you'd be finished! . . .

We had to watch out for cops, too, but we knew quite a few of them. Some of the best customers we had were cops. Sometimes they'd pay for their drinks but mostly we'd take care of them, you know, if they were working the beat. . . . Everyone was on the take back then, all the way up to the mayor, Jimmy Walker. In fact we used to make deliveries to his house every week."

to make wine at home but did not grow their own grapes. California grape growers produced and marketed wine bricks, a solid block of grape concentrate about the size of a pound of butter. Instructions told the purchaser how much water to add to dissolve it into liquid, and "warned" that fermenting would occur if the product sat around too long. Another product called Vine-Glo, which resembled grape jelly, could be mixed with water and put in the cellar for two months; it yielded fairly good wine as well.

Speakeasies and Blind Pigs

While many people drank in the privacy of their own homes, others preferred to defy the law and go out to speakeasies. These illegal drinking spots sprang up in astonishing numbers after the government closed down traditional bars and saloons in 1920. Two years after Prohibition started, New York City had more than 32,000 speakeasies serving the public. Detroit had at least 15,000. A moderate estimate of the total number throughout the nation was over 200,000.

The term "speakeasy" probably came from the Irish "speak softly shop," an illegal tavern or pub where patrons were asked to "speak easy" so that business establishments next door could not hear what was going on. The term might also have referred to the fact that a person had to whisper a code word to the doorman in order to get inside. Whatever the origin, speakeasies were secret places set up in basements, attics, warehouses, and apartment houses. They usually lay behind

Speakeasy doormen sometimes required secret codewords from possible patrons.

within, a dozen or so cigar shops where cigars are grudgingly sold, a vegetarian restaurant, and a real estate office.[116]

Blind pigs were often small, dingy, and crowded. Nightclubs, on the other hand, another type of speakeasy, were usually roomier and offered food, music, and dancing. They, too, operated behind locked doors, and patrons had to show a membership card or be personally introduced before they could enter. Everyone except Prohibition agents or policemen was eligible for membership. Nightclubs generally had decorous names like the "Club Maxine," "Le Basque," and the "Cotton Club"; casual speakeasies had more lively titles like "Mae's Place" and "Jack's Filling Station."

Both men and women enjoyed going to speakeasies and nightclubs because of their warm, friendly atmosphere and because they provided entertainment. The fact that they were illegal and were sometimes raided by the police only made them more attractive. One man had fond memories of his favorite "speak":

locked doors with peepholes, and they always had a lookout who was on the alert for Prohibition agents. Careful owners kept their stock of alcohol out of sight and equipped their rooms with an alarm system that notified them when the police were on the way.

A blind pig was a type of speakeasy that was usually hidden behind a legitimate business such as a grocery store or bowling alley. One man described the blind pigs in his neighborhood:

> They operate under an engaging variety of disguises; a bakery where one may obtain a superb glass of lager, a dry cleaner and pressing establishment where a solid phalanx [barrier] of garments in the window effectively conceals the festivities

> It was in a basement, and that underground feeling, first of all, gave it a fine illegal flavor. . . . The room was rectangle, the walls of it whitewashed brick. At one end was a bar. There were low booths around the walls. There were tables and chairs in the center, red checked tablecloths on the tables. On one side of the room was a low platform on which an orchestra could sit. . . . It was always clean and fairly orderly and very much like a hundred joints today except for the fact that a very fine class of people patronized it and that it was always noisier and friendlier than any places are or ever have been since Prohibition ended.[117]

Some of the most famous speakeasies of the time were those owned by Mary Louise "Tex" Guinan, a blond bombshell who wore diamonds and furs, carried a police whistle, and delighted customers with her caustic humor. Tex was a former silent-movie star who ran speaks in New York and Chicago. In her clubs, respectable people could rub shoulders with politicians, celebrities, and gangsters; spend $25 a bottle for "champagne" (sparkling cider laced with alcohol); and listen to Tex greet everyone with her favorite phrase, "Hello, sucker!"[118]

"Tex" Guinan steps into a paddy wagon after being arrested. The former silent-movie actress owned speakeasies that were frequented by celebrities, politicians, and gangsters.

Actors Rudolph Valentino and John Barrymore patronized Tex's clubs. So did gossip columnist Walter Winchell, who hoped to pick up news tidbits for his readers. When agents raided one of her clubs, Tex simply moved to another, and her clashes with the law often made front-page news. "I like your cute little jail," she told police after a night in the West 30th Street station. "I don't know when my jewels have seemed so safe."[119]

Boiled as an Owl

All the drinking and drunkenness of the twenties gave rise to many slang terms to describe the condition. People could be "boiled as an owl," "lit up like a store window," potted, piped, squiffy, or stinko. Someone on a drinking binge was "on a toot," a shot of alcohol was "hair of the dog," and an empty beer bottle was a "dead soldier."

It was so easy to get liquor during Prohibition that one federal agent timed how long it took him to make an illegal purchase in various cities. New Orleans set the record at thirty-five seconds. All the agent had to do was hop in a taxi and ask the driver where he could buy a drink, and the driver produced a bottle. Detroit followed at three minutes, and New York at three minutes and ten seconds. In only one city—Washington, D.C.—did it take longer than an hour to purchase alcohol, and there a helpful policeman finally directed the agent to a speakeasy.

People used all kinds of devious methods to carry around the forbidden liquor. Hip flasks were so common that jewelry stores produced them in silver, gold, and decorated with jewels. Boots became a popular style for women because a flask could be slipped down the tops. Liquor was also hidden in hollowed-out books, in coconuts, under babies

A flapper displays an ankle flask she has hidden in her boot. People devised all sorts of methods for hiding alcohol.

in buggies, and in hollow canes. One man was caught with two cartons of eggs, all of which had been drained and refilled with liquor.

The Enforcers

Drinkers, speakeasy owners, moonshiners, and bootleggers were constantly on the lookout for Prohibition agents, men hired by the federal government to enforce the drinking ban across the United States. From the beginning, the job of enforcement was extremely difficult. Thousands of agents would have been needed to adequately patrol America's miles of coastline. Thousands more would

have been required to guard its long borders with Canada and Mexico, to scrutinize industries that legally used alcohol and could thereby abuse it, and to uncover the millions of stills that operated throughout the country.

The government had been confident that Americans would cooperate with the law, so it had not budgeted money to combat widespread lawbreaking. It could only afford to hire 1,550 agents, and these were overworked, poorly trained, and poorly paid. Garbage collectors made more money than the agents. The turnover rate for agents was high, and many were fired for taking bribes, falsifying records, committing perjury, and other violations of Prohibition.

The police, who should have provided valuable support to the agents because they were familiar with local neighborhoods, were often willing to look the other way if offered regular bribes. Others extorted money from bootleggers in exchange for silence. One Chicago police officer remembered sniffing out the pungent odor of stills as he and his partner worked their beat. "We were looking for some dough,"[120] he said. During the height of Prohibition, Chicago police chief Charles Fitzmorris admitted that 60 percent of his men were either taking bribes or involved in the bootleg business in some way.

Though many members of law enforcement were lax in enforcing Prohibition, others were overzealous in their efforts to keep the country dry. Many made illegal searches without warrants. Others bullied innocent people, sometimes frightening them into trying to escape and then shooting them. Sometimes, innocent bystanders were struck by flying bullets. One author recounts,

> In many parts of the country, particularly along the Canadian and Mexican borders, there was so much indiscriminate shoot-

ing by prohibition officers that respectable citizens were afraid to drive their automobiles at night. Frequently squads of agents set up roadblocks and searched all cars, without warrant or authority; many citizens who resented such illegal and high-handed procedures were shot.[121]

Prohibition gave law enforcement a bad reputation, but many agents and police officers were conscientious and sincere. In 1921, they shut down more than 95,000 illegal distilleries and stills; in 1930, they raised the numbers to over 282,000. Their job was a frustrating one, however. As quickly as they closed down a speakeasy, a new one popped up farther down the street. If they arrested a bootlegger, his family or henchmen took over his work. In time, even honest, well-intentioned officers and agents became discouraged and doubted that Prohibition could ever be made to work. Their discouragement worsened when their efforts led to tragedies such as the one that occurred on April 8, 1929, in Aurora, Illinois.

On that day, a deputy sheriff went to serve a search warrant on a suspected bootlegger. The bootlegger refused to let the sheriff enter his home, and reinforcements were called in. When the house was stormed, the bootlegger's wife was accidentally shot and killed. Her twelve-year-old son reacted by shooting the sheriff in the leg. Only one gallon of wine was found in the house, causing the sheriff to say from his hospital bed, "I wish there was no such thing as Prohibition. I'm through with it. Try to enforce the law and see what happens."[122]

Izzy and Moe

Two of the most effective Prohibition agents ever to walk the streets of New York City were Isadore "Izzy" Einstein and Moe Smith, a couple of unimpressive looking men who were without equal when it came to catching lawbreakers. Middle-aged, balding Izzy was five foot six and weighed 250 pounds. Moe was a little taller, but weighed more. Because bootleggers were on the lookout for official-looking strangers, the two used an undercover approach. They disguised themselves as waiters, gravediggers, football players, even pickle salesmen, walked into speakeasies and ordered drinks, and then arrested those who sold them liquor. "The main thing, it seems to me," Izzy observed, "is that you have to be natural. The hardest thing an agent has to do is to really act as if he wanted and needed a drink."[123]

Izzy and Moe served as agents for five years. Ironically, they were fired "for the good of the service" on November 13, 1925. Administrators believed their sometimes-clownish antics cast Prohibition agents in a ridiculous light. "The service must be dignified. Izzy and Moe belong on the vaudeville stage,"[124] an official explained. Nevertheless, they were recognized as being responsible for 20 percent of all the New York Prohibition cases that came to trial during their term of service. After he finished his stint with the government, Izzy wrote his memoirs, dedicated to "the 4,932 persons I arrested, hoping they bear me no grudge for having done my duty."[125]

Eliot Ness and the Untouchables

Prohibition agent Eliot Ness was more serious than Izzy and Moe, but he was just as dedicated and effective. Tall, handsome, and well educated, Ness began his alcohol-fighting career in Chicago in 1927. A short time later, he was put in charge of closing down Al Capone's enormous bootlegging enterprises in the city.

Despite their ridiculous antics, agents Izzy Einstein (left) and Moe Smith were extremely effective at catching Prohibition violators.

Ness and his nine-man team of "Untouchables" soon gained a reputation for being incorruptible as well as fearless. They had to be. Capone was the most powerful mobster of the time and did not hesitate to kill anyone who opposed him. "I felt a chill of foreboding for my men as I envisioned the violent reaction we would produce in the criminal octopus hovering over Chicago," Ness wrote. "We had undertaken what might be a suicidal mission."[126]

Over the course of four years, Ness and his men smashed stills, closed down breweries, and narrowly escaped assassination. Although the Untouchables had nothing to do with bringing Capone to justice, they did make a significant impact on the gangster's liquor business, and Ness was on hand to escort Capone to the train that carried him to prison in 1932.

A Lawless Business

Supporters of Prohibition like Izzy, Moe, and Eliot Ness were sincere in their belief that the law—if enforced effectively—would improve

Einstein, Rum Sleuth

The comical appearance of Izzy Einstein and Moe Smith belied their commitment to enforcing Prohibition. On March 26, 1922, the *New York Times* carried an article on Einstein that highlighted the skill and creativity he brought to his job. The article is included in *The Twenties: Fords, Flappers, and Fanatics*, edited by George E. Mowry.

"Izzy one evening walked into the Yorkville Casino with a trombone under his arm. The false-front shirt, Ascot tie and other infallible markings of the orchestra musician were upon him. He could play the trombone, too, just as on a similar occasion in Brooklyn he utilized a violin to win over the restaurant management. . . . In each instance the charm of his music brought proffers of drinks, which he accepted, and then displayed his gratitude by distributing summonses. . . .

Izzy can drive a truck as well as he can guide a push cart. And trucks bear a definite relation to bootlegging. . . . Izzy mastered trucking and on occasions too numerous to recount he has in his capacity of chauffeur driven many a load of his unsuspecting employer's booze straight to a Government warehouse. And not only the immediate load, but all the rest of the supply from which it came. . . .

As a pickle salesman, Izzy trapped many a saloon owner and grocer who thought the drummer's [salesman's] reasonable prices warranted a return favor. In one instance Izzy's low pickle prices prompted the trusting grocer to offer him a drink of his best Scotch, also at a price correspondingly reduced—and the grocer at once suffered the consequences."

society. Other Americans, however, became disillusioned as the decade wore on. Writer H.L. Mencken stated, "All that the Prohibitionists have accomplished by their holy crusade is to augment vastly the number of boozers in the United States, and to convert the trade in alcohol, once a lawful business, into a criminal racket."[127]

That "racket," and other illegal activities of criminals like Al Capone, marked the worst of the twenties and contributed to its reputation as an age of lawlessness.

Americans grumbled about what they saw as a massive increase in crime in the 1920s. There were plenty of articles about gangsters, racketeers, and big-time swindlers who thumbed their noses at law enforcement. Even ordinary citizens seemed inclined to break the law when it served their purpose.

Statistics showed, however, that national crime rates for burglary, robbery, and even murder were not significantly higher than they had been in earlier times. Cities such as Chicago were notorious for their killing and corruption, but a great deal of the lawbreaking related to Prohibition. Most people led peaceful, respectable lives and only read about swindles, murders, and gangland activities in the news, finding a certain amount of adventure and romance in the articles. "The gangster was an exotic [figure], seldom seen, only talked about,"[128] writes one author.

The Great Swindler

Charles Ponzi was one of the swindlers people read about in their morning newspapers. The Great Ponzi, as he called himself, dreamed of being a financier, but he was just a clerk at J.P. Poole, a foreign trade house in Boston. In 1919, however, he left that job and formed the Old Colony Foreign Exchange Company, advertising that he could buy a type of international money order at a low price in one country and then sell it a short time later in another country, making a profit by taking advantage of favorable exchange rates. Ponzi promised to pay $15 for every $10 that investors left in his care.

Within six months, Ponzi was taking in $1 million a week from investors who probably suspected that his scheme was shady but wanted to get rich quick. As the money began to roll in, Ponzi actually seemed to be distributing profits. In fact, he was just shuffling money from new investors to old ones. Using a sizable chunk of his proceeds, he bought himself a big house and a chauffeured limousine. He took over J.P. Poole and fired his former boss. He lived the good life.

In 1920, authorities discovered that the Old Colony Exchange was a fraud and arrested Ponzi. Despite the fact that he had swindled his customers, some still admired him. "You're the greatest Italian of them all!" one shouted to him on his way to jail. Ponzi modestly protested, "No, no. Columbus and Marconi. Columbus discovered America. Marconi discovered the wireless." "So what?" his admirer said. "You discovered money."[129]

"Buy Anywhere, You Can't Lose"

When Ponzi got out of jail, he unsuccessfully tried his hand at another dubious scheme— land speculation. He was not alone. All across the country, cities were growing, the surrounding countryside was being divided into subdivisions, and anyone who could afford to buy undeveloped land in a reasonable location was sure of being able to sell it in the near future for a profit.

In the early 1920s, Florida was the state of choice when it came to speculating on land. Past investors had been highly successful. In 1896, a man named C.W. Bingham bought oceanfront property at Palm Beach (which was then nothing but windswept sand) for $4.65 a frontage foot. By 1925, it was selling for $3,300 a frontage foot. Before World War I, investor Carl G. Fisher bought swamp and jungle land for next to nothing, then drained it, built up the beach, and helped pave the way for the city of Miami. Fisher reportedly made nearly $40 million selling lots.

There were other advantages to buying in Florida. It had clean air, white sand, and blue ocean. The weather was warm. It was within driving distance for people in the East who wanted a winter getaway. And it was not far from "wet" Caribbean islands where good liquor could be easily obtained. By 1925, the

Charles Ponzi became wealthy from a get-rich-quick scheme, illegally swindling people out of their money.

When land speculation in Florida hit its height in the summer of 1925, the once-sleepy town of Miami was the center of the hoopla. Historian Frederick Lewis Allen describes the excited goings-on in *Only Yesterday: An Informal History of the 1920's.*

"There was nothing languorous [slow and sleepy] about the atmosphere of tropical Miami during that memorable summer and autumn of 1925. The whole city had become one frenzied real-estate exchange. There were said to be 2,000 real-estate offices and 25,000 agents marketing house-lots or acreage. The shirt-sleeved crowds hurrying to and fro under the widely adver-

tised Florida sun talked of binders and options and water-frontages and hundred-thousand-dollar profits; the city fathers had been forced to pass an ordinance forbidding the sale of property in the street, or even the showing of a map, to prevent inordinate traffic congestion. . . . Motor-busses roared down Flagler Street, carrying 'prospects' on free trips to watch dredges and steam-shovels converting the outlying mangrove swamps . . . into gorgeous Venetian cities for the American homemakers and pleasure-seekers of the future. The Dixie Highway was clogged with automobiles from every part of the country; a traveler caught in a traffic jam counted the license-plates of eighteen states among the sedans and flivvers waiting in line. . . . The public utilities of the city were trying desperately to meet the suddenly multiplied demand for electricity and gas and telephone service, and there were recurrent shortages of ice."

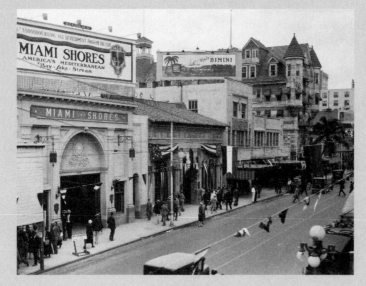

A view of Flagler Street in Miami during the height of the Florida real-estate boom.

state was in the midst of speculation fever, and doctors, lawyers, shop owners, and retired people headed south, looking for a good investment.

Miami was the center of the action, and real estate salesmen were everywhere. A person could buy land from someone on a street corner, and many did, making their purchases after consulting only a blueprint or a sketch. Free bus trips were available for those who wanted to actually see what they were buying, and thousands took advantage of that option.

Buying land was extremely easy. There were no title investigations and no deeds recorded. For a simple 10 percent down payment—known as a binder—anyone could reserve the lot of their choice. Buying and selling binders became as popular as dealing with real estate itself.

Even for the sensible, the lure of making a fast dollar was often too strong to pass up. One journalist who went to Florida to write about the frenzy yielded to temptation and paid $2,500 for a binder. She then sold it for a profit before the month was over. She wrote, "Joining the great migration this summer, I went inclined to scoff. . . . I confess—not brag—that on a piker's [miserly] purchase I made in a month about $13,000. Not much, perhaps, but a lot to a little buyer on a little bet."[130]

Of course, there were swindles. Unscrupulous salespeople sold land that turned out to be in a swamp or even underwater. Some sold binders on land that did not exist. A man named Ben Hecht faked the discovery of hidden pirate treasure in the Key Largo area, and people flocked to buy there. The motto was "Buy anywhere, you can't lose,"[131] and people believed the hype.

By 1926, some of the "get rich quick" glow had begun to fade. Many speculators had not been able to sell their binders at the high price they expected. Some could not make follow-up payments on their property and had to forfeit. Land came back to original owners with taxes and assessments due.

Then disaster struck. Two hurricanes blew across southern Florida in quick succession. The second wiped out towns, killed four hundred people, injured over six thousand, and left almost fifty thousand homeless. Suddenly, Florida was not the glorious getaway that it had once seemed, and Florida land was not the best of investments. The speculation balloon collapsed, leaving thousands facing debt, bankruptcies, and foreclosures. It also left them a little wiser. One author writes, "The hurricane of 1926 had blown away . . . the

Miami's ravaged coastline following the 1926 hurricane that dealt a disastrous blow to land speculation in Florida.

illusion that there would always be another sucker who would come along, buy you out, make you rich, and be left holding the bag."[132]

Big-Time Crime

Florida realtors and crooked characters like Charles Ponzi were insignificant threats when compared to bigger criminals that reigned supreme during the twenties. Gangsters who were involved in organized crime such as gambling, prostitution, and drug running had always played a role in city life, but none had been as brazen as those that came to power during Prohibition. Realizing that there were millions to be made from illegal liquor, they bought out beer breweries, hijacked each other's liquor, paid police to look the other way, and intimidated speakeasy owners into buying their booze. "All I've done is supply a public demand," rationalized Al Capone. "They say I violate the prohibition law. Who doesn't?"[133]

Most of the gangster activity took place in big cities. A group called the Purple Gang controlled crime in Detroit. St. Louis, Missouri, had Egan's Rats. In Philadelphia, Maxie Hoff was head man. Some of New York City's most infamous gangsters were Dutch Schultz, Owney Madden, and Frankie Yale.

Chicago was the center of gangland activities, however, and the most notorious gangster of them all was Al "Scarface" Capone. In the words of one observer, he was "a big fat man with a cigar and a $50,000 pinkie ring. A jowly smiling Satan . . . with two scars across his left cheek. He weighed over two-fifty, yet despite his bulk and the sloppy grin, he could move with lethal speed and force. Not an articulate man, he was nonetheless charismatic: warm, charming, generous. A big tipper."[134]

Big Al

Big Al, as he was also known, came to Chicago in about 1920, after underworld figure Johnny Torrio asked the twenty-three-year-old hoodlum to join him there and help him run his crime empire. The young Capone proved to be a talented and capable administrator. Under the noses of respectable citizens, he used a combination of payoffs, threats, and violence to gain control of police and politicians as well as brothels, speakeasies, gambling dens, and breweries. Chicago soon gained a reputation as the most corrupt city in the nation.

After Torrio retired in 1925, Capone took over his empire. So tight was the gangster's hold on the city that he could walk the

Chicago gang leader Al "Scarface" Capone was the most dangerous and notorious of the Prohibition-era gangsters.

Street-Side Shooting Gallery

Until about 1926, gangsters relied on pistols, shotguns, and homemade bombs in their violent dealings with one another. After submachine guns made their way onto the black market and into gang members' hands, however, a new approach to gangster warfare developed. In *Only Yesterday: An Informal History of the 1920's*, Frederick Lewis Allen describes the first of many scenes that became almost common in Chicago in the twenties.

"In 1926 the O'Banions . . . introduced another novelty in gang warfare. In broad daylight, while the streets of Cicero [a Chicago suburb] were alive with traffic, they raked Al Capone's headquarters with machinegun fire from eight touring cars. The cars proceeded down the crowded street outside the Hawthorne Hotel in solemn line, the first one firing blank cartridges to disperse the innocent citizenry and to draw the Capone forces to the doors and windows, while from the succeeding cars, which followed a block behind, flowed a steady rattle of bullets, spraying the hotel and the adjoining buildings up and down. One gunman even got out of his car, knelt carefully upon the sidewalk at the door of the Hawthorne, and played one hundred bullets into the lobby—back and forth, as one might play the hose upon one's garden. The casualties were miraculously light, and Scarface Al himself remained in safety, flat on the floor of the Hotel Hawthorne restaurant; nevertheless, the bombardment quite naturally attracted public attention. Even in a day when bullion [gold] was transported in armored cars, the transformation of a suburban street into a shooting-gallery seemed a little unorthodox."

---

streets with impunity. At one point, a city official asked Capone, rather than the police, to ensure that the local elections took place without violence or intimidation from other gangs. "Capone is the most dangerous, the most resourceful, the most cruel, the most menacing, the most conscienceless of any criminal of modern times," stated Henry Barret Chamberlin, a member of the Chicago Crime Commission, formed in 1919. "He has contributed more to besmirch the fair name of Chicago than any man living or dead."[135]

Killing was second nature to Capone, just as it was to all gangsters. He killed to intimidate and teach people a lesson. He killed for revenge. Sometimes he had his men get rid of an enemy by taking him "for a ride" out to a deserted spot where he was shot and his body tossed in a ditch. Sometimes shootings occurred in broad daylight, as if to emphasize the killers' fearlessness. One historian also notes, "One of the standard methods of disposing of a rival . . . was to pursue his car with a stolen automobile full of men armed with sawed-off shotguns and submachine guns; to draw up beside it, forcing it to the curb, open fire upon it—and then disappear into the traffic."[136]

Not surprisingly, innocent people who happened to be in the wrong place at the wrong time were sometimes hurt during drive-by shootings. Waiters and maitre-d's in restaurants were prepared to drop to the floor when bullets came flying. Passersby were not always so wary. In one shootout in which Capone narrowly avoided death, several bullets struck the Freeman family, who happened to be driving by in their car. Five-year-old Clyde Jr. was shot in the knee, and Anna Freeman received a bullet in her arm and a shard of glass from the shattered windshield in her eye. Capone generously insisted on paying their medical expenses, which totaled $10,000. One of his men explained, "The Big Fellow never wants bystanders hurt."[137]

Mom, Pop, and the "Gorillas"

Most ordinary people did not fear being shot by a gangster as they went about their daily lives. Even if they visited a speakeasy or a gambling den, their contact was usually limited to bartenders, card dealers, and other customers. There was always the danger that someone could be caught in the midst of a shootout, but since those did not occur every day, the risks were slight.

When it came to racketeering, however, the odds changed. Racketeering was the criminal practice of controlling businesses and labor unions and extorting money from them using threats and violence. It touched thousands of lives. Most racketeers were less powerful than gangsters like Al Capone (who was himself a racketeer), but they were lawbreakers who could be just as frightening.

Some racketeers were labor union organizers. Others were merely tough guys who intimidated small businessmen by throwing bricks through their windows, beating them up, or possibly murdering one of them as an example to others. The threat of future violence forced businessmen to join "protective associations" headed by racketeers. A 1927

The High Cost of Hoodlums

Racketeering was not a new form of crime in the United States, but it reached new heights in the 1920s, especially in cities such as Chicago and New York. Author John Gunther points out the cost of racketeering for the ordinary Chicagoan in a 1929 article included in *The Twenties: Fords, Flappers, and Fanatics*, edited by George E. Mowry.

"Crime is affecting the Chicago citizen in a new fashion. A system of criminal exploitation, based on extortion, controlled by hoodlums, and decorated with icy-cold murder, has arisen in the past five or six years, to seize the ordinary Chicagoan, you and me and the man across the street, by the pocket-book if not the throat. Crime is costing me money. It is costing money to the taxi-driver who took me to the office this morning, the elevator boy who lifted me ten stories through the steel stratifications of a great skyscraper, the waiter who served me my luncheon, the suburban business man who sat at the next table. Very few persons, in Chicago or out of it, realize how this criminal system works. Very few persons, in Chicago or out of it, realize that the ordinary citizen is paying literal tribute to racketeers. This tribute is levied in many ways. The ordinary citizen pays it, . . . whenever he has a suit pressed and every time he gets a haircut; he may pay it in the plumbing in his house and the garaging of his car; the very garbage behind his back door may perhaps mean spoil for someone."

edition of the *Chicago Journal of Commerce* explained what followed:

> [The racketeer] then proceeds to collect what fees and dues he likes, to impose what fines suit him, regulates price and hours of work, and . . . to boss the outfit to his own profit. Any merchant who doesn't come in, or who comes in and doesn't stay in and continue to pay tribute, is bombed, slugged or otherwise intimidated.[138]

In cities controlled by racketeers, honest competition was almost impossible. Prices were set, and no one could operate a business without paying protection money. Even small "mom and pop" operations lived in fear of a visit from a thug who would come into their shop and let them know they had to conform to the boss's demands or pay the price.

The rackets controlled businesses such as dry cleaners, fish vendors, garbage removal, drugstores, florists, shoe repair shops, and photographers. Chicago had an estimated ninety rackets. Ordinary people bemoaned the scope of the problem, but racketeers argued that the entire country was a series of rackets. One historian paraphrased their rationale: "What was the insurance business but a giant racket, and a legal one at that? What was John D. Rockefeller's Standard Oil monopoly but the most lucrative racket in the country, and Rockefeller himself the biggest racketeer of them all?"[139] It was all a matter of perspective, and those who were involved in crime were inclined to see everyone as being as corrupt as themselves.

All Eyes on Murder

In 1930, after exhaustive efforts by the federal government to amass evidence against Al

Al Capone (center) being led from Chicago Federal Court after receiving an eleven-year sentence for income tax evasion.

Capone, the gang leader was brought to trial. Under the stern eye of Judge James H. Wilkerson, he was found guilty, not of murder, bootlegging, or racketeering but of failure to file his tax returns. Capone was sentenced to eleven years in prison. "I'm not sore at anybody," he said on his way to the federal penitentiary in Atlanta, Georgia. "Some people are lucky. I wasn't."[140]

Al Capone's trial was notable, but it was not the only one to capture America's attention in the twenties. There were other cases that were followed with equal or greater interest. One that involved forbidden passion and the church was the double murder of the Reverend Edward W. Hall and Eleanor Mills, a singer in the church choir. On September 14, 1922, the two were found dead in an abandoned orchard near their homes in New

Brunswick, New Jersey. Scattered between the bodies were their torn-up love letters. Hall had been shot once. Mills had been shot three times in the head, and her tongue and larynx had been cut out.

Many people in the neighborhood knew that the couple had been lovers, and there had been rumors that they were going to elope in the near future. Logical suspects in the murder were the wronged husband; Reverend Hall's wife; Mrs. Hall's mentally retarded brother, Willie, who owned a gun of the same caliber as the murder weapon; and another brother Henry, who was an expert shot. But there were other suspects as well. Even the Ku Klux Klan was suspected of having executed the couple for their immoral acts.

The investigation was mismanaged and became so confused that police and prosecutors allowed the case to grow cold. Then, in 1926, William Randolph Hearst's *Daily Mirror*, eager to increase its circulation, pushed for a reopening of the case. It claimed that new evidence had emerged, including the eyewitness testimony of an eccentric New Brunswick woman, Mrs. Jane Gibson, who raised pigs. Gibson stated that she had seen Mrs. Hall's cousin Henry Carpender kill Reverend Hall and Eleanor Mills in the apple orchard. She claimed that Mrs. Hall and her brothers, Willie and Henry, had been present.

While the nation followed the story, the four were arrested and brought to trial. Gibson, who the tabloids had nicknamed the "Pig Woman," was dying of cancer and had to be carried in to court on a stretcher in order to testify. After a grueling cross-examination, she looked toward the defendants and stated, "I've told the truth so help me God and you know I've told the truth."[141]

The jury was not convinced, however. Gibson had told her story to the newspapers in 1922, and the details of her later testimony did not match the earlier account. People also noted that she was not as ill as she had led the court to believe. (Despite the fact that she had appeared to be at death's door at the trial, she lived for four more years.) The jury acquitted the defendants, and the case remained unsolved.

Murder for Kicks

A more gruesome murder that occurred in Indiana in 1924 fascinated the country because it involved youth, wealth, and abnormal psychology. On May 22 of that year, the naked, acid-burned body of fourteen-year-old Robert Franks was discovered stuffed into a concrete culvert just outside the town of Hammond. Nine days later, two local teens confessed to the crime. The details, when revealed, left the nation aghast at the killers' arrogance and brutality. Just as disturbing was the fact that neither of them fit the stereotype of what everyone thought a typical criminal should be—poor, powerless, and stupid.

Nathan Leopold, age nineteen, and Richard Loeb, eighteen, were two highly intelligent college men. Leopold had entered the University of Chicago at the age of fourteen, graduated with high honors, and spoke five languages fluently. Loeb had just graduated from the University of Michigan, getting his degree in just over two years. Coming from wealthy backgrounds, both men had parents who gave them too many material things and too little love. The two brought out the worst in each other and eventually convinced themselves that they were supermen, above the laws that applied to ordinary beings.

As time passed, the pair decided to pull off the perfect kidnapping. They chose young Robert Franks at random and lured him into a car. Loeb then impulsively killed the boy by

The nation was shocked when wealthy college students Nathan Leopold (left) and Richard Loeb confessed to the gruesome murder of fourteen-year-old Robert Franks.

bashing in his skull with a chisel. Murder had not been part of their plan, but both Leopold and Loeb took it in stride. "Anything is justifiable in the interest of science," a tabloid reported Leopold as saying. "It is no crime to use a human being in the interest of scientific research. It is no more than impaling a beetle on a pin."[142] Before stuffing the body in the drainpipe, Leopold doused it with acid to disguise its identity.

Darrow for the Defense

Because they had confessed, the fate of Leopold and Loeb was sealed. Having been judged sane, they faced life imprisonment or death. Their parents hired one of the top criminal attorneys in the country, Clarence Darrow, in an attempt to save their lives. Darrow decided to focus the trial on the condition of his clients' minds. He relied on the latest in modern science when preparing their defense.

Darrow called in psychologists who cited Freudian theories and testified that Leopold and Loeb had been motivated to commit murder because of unconscious desires or impulses beyond their control. Darrow also introduced medical experts who explained that physical and chemical imbalances caused by the endocrine glands could cause disease or personality change. This was based on a theory known at the time as "glandism." "We are not going to introduce evidence of insanity," Darrow stated, "but we do intend to show that our clients are mentally diseased."[143]

The experts testified that both young men had physical abnormalities that could account for their criminal thinking. In Leopold's case, they stated that "there had been a premature involution of the thymus gland and a premature calcification of the pineal gland in the skull; that the pituitary gland was overactive; and that the adrenal glands did not function normally."[144]

Darrow also demonstrated that both young men had had negative experiences

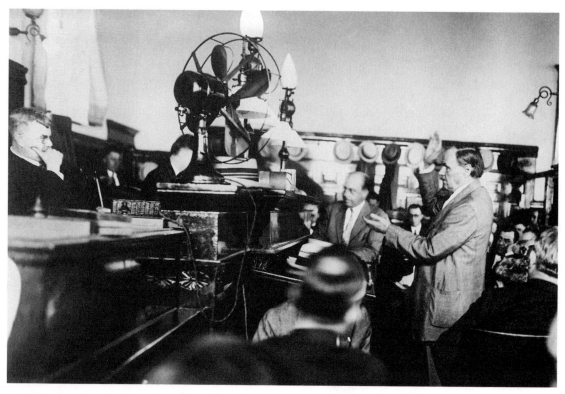

Defense attorney Clarence Darrow (right) argues before the judge during the trial of Leopold and Loeb.

early in their lives that had affected their emotional development. Leopold's mother had died when he was young. Loeb had been raised by a tyrannical governess. Darrow maintained, "I know that they cannot feel what you feel and what I feel, that they cannot feel the moral shocks which come to men that are educated and who have not been deprived of an emotional system or emotional feelings."[145]

"Redemption Is Sometimes Possible"

On the day Darrow was scheduled to give his closing arguments, large crowds waited to get in the courtroom. The attorney was well known, and everyone expected his final summation to be memorable. They also wanted to see if Leopold and Loeb would have to die for their crime. As the doors to the courtroom opened, one journalist reported, "The tidal wave of men and women swept over and flattened a skirmish line of bailiffs at the main entrance and poured up the stairs and the elevators, sweeping all obstacles away."[146]

Their fervor was justified. Darrow spoke for more than twelve hours during the next three days, emphasizing his clients' upbringing and their youthfulness. A strong opponent of capital punishment, he reminded the judge that the young men's execution could hurt the nation rather than help it. "I tell you, civilization will be dealt a terrible blow if these boys hang. We will be turning back to the days when they burned children at the stake,"[147] he insisted. His speech was so moving that several members of the audience were crying when he finished.

Darrow's eloquence did not win his clients their freedom, but it did persuade the judge to spare their lives. Both were sentenced to life in prison. There, Loeb was murdered by another prisoner in 1936.

Leopold's story ended differently. A model prisoner, he spent thirty-three years reclassifying the prison library, writing his autobiography, and working in an experimental program to find a cure for malaria. He was paroled in 1958 and moved to Puerto Rico, where he married, earned a master's degree, and did research on leprosy. When Leopold died in 1971, the *Chicago Sun-Times* made a point of noting that at least one of the wrongdoers of the twenties had done his best to make amends for his crimes: "Three lives were lost in that long-ago moment of youthful madness. Justice was served. And the only saving feature was that one of the killers was able, in a small way, to prove that redemption is sometimes possible."[148]

Whether redeemable or not, criminals like Al Capone and Leopold and Loeb served to reinforce many Americans' beliefs that modern society fostered evil. In their opinion, something needed to be done to counteract modern trends. Through movements like Christian fundamentalism and the Ku Klux Klan, they stepped out, spoke up, and did what they believed needed to be done to make changes for the better. The trouble and controversy they stirred up in the process, however, only added to the twenties' reputation as a decade of extremes.

The Monkey Trial and the Invisible Empire

Despite the public's fascination with sex, murder, and the criminal world, most Americans in small towns and rural areas held tight to their conservative roots in the '20s. They believed in God, the flag, and Prohibition, and they condemned the materialism and modern morals that were showcased on the radio and in magazines and newspapers.

Intolerance was common among this segment of society. They were wary of anyone who was "different," including blacks, immigrants, and liberals. In one midwestern town with few minorities, an observer noted,

> The small group of foreign-born mingle little with the rest of the community. Negroes are allowed under protest in the schools but not in the larger motion picture houses or in Y.M.C.A. . . . They are not to be found in "white" churches; Negro children must play in their own restricted corner of the Park.[149]

The Fundamentalists

Intolerance was often reflected in religious attitudes, with Jews and Catholics being particularly unpopular. "Membership in one of the religious groups is generally taken for granted, particularly among the business class, and a newcomer is commonly greeted with the question, 'What church do you go to?'"[150] said one observer. Those who did not answer "Baptist," "Methodist," or one of the other Protestant denominations were looked at with suspicion and disapproval.

A growing fundamentalist movement, made up of the most conservative members of Protestant groups, contributed to the intolerant mood. Fundamentalist Christians believed that events in the Bible had to be interpreted literally. For instance, they insisted that God created the earth in six, twenty-four-hour days; that Adam was the first human being on earth; and that Eve was created out of Adam's rib. They rejected other points of view and claims of modern science that the earth was billions of years old, that cavemen preceded modern man, and the like. They were particularly offended by Charles Darwin's theory of evolution, which claims that all related organisms share common ancestors and that human beings are descendants of apes.

Fundamentalists believed that God wanted them to fight against attitudes and behavior that might weaken Christianity and society. "We are in the midst of a period of criticism in which certain so-called 'intellectuals' are trying to destroy the Bible and men's faith in the fundamentals of Christianity, but the Bible still stands,"[151] said the representative of one church. Churches held well-attended meetings to discuss strategies for combating immoral trends. Ministers spoke against sin and science from the pulpit. At school board meetings, at town councils, and in newspaper editorials, ordinary citizens urged a return to traditional values.

Billy and Aimee

Two of the most well known and influential fundamentalists of the time were Billy Sunday and Aimee Semple McPherson. Sunday had been a professional baseball player in his youth. He then became an ordained Presbyterian minister who led revivals—evangelistic meetings held in huge tents at various locales around the country. During revival meetings, Sunday stirred his audience into an emotional fervor, exhorted them to turn away from their sins, and encouraged them to win others for Christ.

Sunday had a dynamic style, and his oratory attracted millions of people. He would shout,

I'm against sin. I'll kick it as long as I've got a foot, and I'll fight it as long as I've got a fist. I'll butt it as long as I've got a head. I'll bite it as long as I've got a tooth. And when I'm old and fistless and footless and toothless, I'll gum it till I go home to Glory and it goes home to perdition [hell]![152]

Many who attended Sunday's meetings took his words to heart and vowed to stand firm

Men peruse fundamentalist books that condemn teaching the theory of evolution in school.

Revival meetings were rallying places for people who wanted to revitalize their faith and bring others to accept Jesus Christ as savior. The meetings were also a form of entertainment, complete with music and dramatic performances by colorful evangelists. One of the most dynamic was former baseball player Billy Sunday, whose style is described in Vivian Baulch's *Detroit News* article "How Billy Sunday Battled Demon Rum in Detroit."

"Attired in a light gray suit and white shoes . . . Sunday feinted, walked and ran, crouched and jumped, from one end of the stage to the other, sweating from his gyrations until he was wet as a rag held under a pump.

By his actions he kept the audience transfixed, hanging upon his every word and movement. He jumped on a chair; down on the floor again. He beat out a cadence with his fist upon the platform in order to emphasize a series of points; on top of the pulpit, he tore off his coat and collar and threw them to the stage. . . .

Wild-eyed at the climax of his address, like an addict going cold turkey, Sunday told his God to help old Detroit [where he was preaching at the time]. Throw your arms around her. Go into her barber shops, Lord, into the hotels, factories, and saloons. Help the man in the street, the floater, and drunkard. The devil has him almost out. He's on the ropes and groggy, Lord. One more stiff uppercut will finish him. Help him, Lord, to square his shoulders, raise his dukes [fists] and cry, 'Yes, Lord, I'll come when Bill gives the call.'"

Fundamentalist minister Billy Sunday stirs up the crowd during one of his fiery sermons.

against even such mild temptations as dancing and playing cards.

Aimee Semple McPherson was just as dramatic as Sunday, but she was a rarity in the twenties—a woman preacher. Her uniqueness was highlighted by her magnetic personality, her angelic appearance (she always wore white flowing robes during services), and her sentimental style. "These are the days of great heartbreaks; these are the days when angels themselves must weep tears over the balustrades of heaven over this old world,"[153] she said.

McPherson reached out to millions of Americans by broadcasting over the radio from her enormous Angelus Temple in Los Angeles. Her colorful services and her sermons emphasizing heaven, happiness, and God's love were popular among people who were used to listening to ministers preaching hellfire and damnation. As one man who listened to her wrote, "Of all the Fundamentalists she is by far the friendliest. She talks of both a literal hell and devil, but only in a nice way. This is not a bonfire to send any of the neurotic into hysterics."[154]

Scandal shook McPherson's ministry when she disappeared in May 1926 while swimming at the beach in Venice, California. Several weeks later she reappeared, claiming she had been kidnapped. Her story was not supported by facts, however, and newspapers printed rumors that she had been seen in a motel with a man during the time she was away. Nevertheless, the faithful of the temple continued to believe in her and her message.

"Before a densely massed congregation of 7,500 persons, Aimee Semple McPherson, the evangelist, today received a thunderous welcome when she returned to her pulpit in Angelus Temple,"[155] the *New York Times* reported after her comeback from her mysterious misadventure.

Darwin vs. the Bible

Billy Sunday, Aimee Semple McPherson, and other fundamentalists were scandalized in the summer of 1925 when the news broke that a Dayton, Tennessee, teacher had taught evolution in his classroom.

John Thomas Scopes was a likable twenty-four-year-old who taught high school biology. He knew that the Tennessee legislature had recently passed the Butler Act, a law prohibiting public schools from teaching any theory that denied the story of creation in the Bible. He also knew that the

Aimee Semple McPherson preaches to a huge crowd in 1928. McPherson gained a following at a time when female preachers were rare.

The Monkey Trial and the Invisible Empire

textbook he used included a section on Darwin, natural selection, and evolution. With the support of the American Civil Liberties Union (ACLU), which believed that the new law violated the First Amendment, Scopes allowed himself to be caught teaching the forbidden subject. He was promptly arrested.

Scopes's trial, nicknamed the "Monkey Trial" by the press, gained national attention for its promise of theatrics. Attorney Clarence Darrow, a renowned agnostic, was part of the defense team. Former presidential candidate and fundamentalist Christian William Jennings Bryan served as prosecutor and dramatically announced that the trial would be a "duel to the death"[156] between Christianity and evolution.

People rushed to quiet little Dayton to see the trial. Evangelists set up a makeshift tabernacle in one locale; shops sold monkey toys; the soda fountain featured a drink called a "monkey fizz"; and the butcher shop hung up a sign that stated, "We handle all kinds of meat except monkey."[157] One author writes, "In the courtroom itself, as the trial impended, reporters and camera men crowded alongside grim-faced Tennessee countrymen; there was . . . an air of suspense like that of a first-night performance at the theater."[158]

Lost Cause

As the proceedings got under way, Bryan had no trouble showing that Scopes had broken the law. There were several teen witnesses who testified that evolution had been taught in their biology class. Darrow, however, was successful in showing that they had not been harmed by the exposure to the illegal theory.

Main Street Hullabaloo

Living in Dayton, Tennessee, during the summer of the Scopes Monkey Trial was a never-to-be-forgotten experience, and Wallace Robinson, son of the town's pharmacist, had a firsthand view of the excitement. His unique perspective is included in Peter Jennings and Todd Brewster's *The Century*.

"Most of the people of Dayton were fundamentalist Christians, but there were quite a few of us who felt otherwise, of course. My father was the county druggist during the time of Scopes. He went in business in 1898, and by 1925, he was chairman of the school board. He sided with Darrow and the evolutionists because he didn't believe that the state or federal government had a right to tell a local school board what they could or could not teach. Like most druggists, my dad was also a purveyor of textbooks, so he was as guilty as Scopes, I guess, in the sense that he had hired Scopes to teach school and was selling the textbook which was in question. Still, he really enjoyed the trial and all the hullabaloo and he saw it as an opportunity to promote the drugstore. . . . We lived less than a hundred yards from the courthouse and they had speakers out on the front lawn, bellowing the trial out to the crowds. . . . The trial was really a hullabaloo. Everywhere we had hucksters selling watch fobs and handmade dolls. When I die, I'll hopefully go to heaven, and I want to ask the Lord, what was it all about?"

Defense attorney Clarence Darrow (left) speaks with chief prosecutor William Jennings Bryan during the famous trial of John Thomas Scopes. Scopes was arrested for teaching evolution in the classroom.

One exchange with seventeen-year-old Harry Sheldon revealed his loyalty to the church to be unshaken:

Q. Did Professor Scopes teach you anything about evolution?

A. He taught that all forms of life begin with the cell. . . .

Q. That's all you remember that he told you about biology, wasn't it?

A. Yes, sir.

Q. Are you a church member?

A. Yes, sir. . . .

Q. You didn't leave when he told you all forms of life began with a single cell?

A. No, sir.[159]

Darrow had hoped to base his fight on constitutional issues—the fact that Tennessee was violating the separation of church and state and was also forbidding the teaching of a widely accepted scientific theory. The judge, who sat under a banner that proclaimed "Read Your Bible," would not allow the jury to hear any of the scientific witnesses the defense attorney planned to introduce, however.

Darrow finally resorted to exposing the intellectual weaknesses of fundamentalism.

In a move that shocked the audience, he asked Bryan to take the stand as an expert witness on the Bible. He then proceeded to ask questions that Bryan and most fundamentalists had difficulty answering: If Adam, Eve, Cain, and Abel were the only people on earth, where had Cain gotten his wife? How had Jonah survived in a fish's stomach for three days? What year had the flood taken place? How many people lived on earth at the beginning of the Christian era?

Bryan was made to look foolish by his lack of knowledge and by his inability to support his point of view with facts or logical arguments. He also made the mistake of stating that a "day" in the Genesis account of creation might have been longer than twenty-four hours. With that admission, he revealed that he himself sometimes did not take the Bible literally. Publicly humiliated, Bryan left the stand. The judge prevented Darrow from continuing the examination the next day.

In spite of his triumph over Bryan, Darrow realized that he was going to lose his case. He decided that his best chance stood with an appeal to a higher court, which would perhaps be less biased. When the trial wrapped up, the jury needed only eight minutes to find Scopes guilty. He was fined $100 for his offense and was fired from his teaching position.

Bryan had won, but he was a broken man. Five days later, he died of complications from diabetes. Darrow appealed the Scopes case and saw the state supreme court reverse the verdict on a technicality. Nevertheless, the court maintained that the Butler Act was constitutional. It remained on the books until 1967.

Sacco and Vanzetti

The Scopes trial highlighted America's religious narrow-mindedness. The case of Nicola Sacco and Bartolomeo Vanzetti demonstrated the lengths the country could go in its unfair treatment of outsiders. An increase in racism and isolationism in the United States after World War I had led to hostility toward immigrants, particularly those from southern and eastern Europe, Russia, and Asia. People from these regions were believed to be inferior to immigrants from northern and western Europe.

On May 5, 1920, Sacco and Vanzetti, two Italian newcomers, were arrested on suspicion of having committed a payroll robbery near South Braintree, Massachusetts, the previous April. During the course of the robbery, a paymaster and his guard had been killed. The suspects, who spoke little English, were in a car that had been connected with the crime. Both men were carrying loaded revolvers. Sacco's was the same caliber as the gun used in the shooting.

Another damning fact was soon uncovered. Both men were members of an anarchist group that was antigovernment and in favor of eliminating all economic, political, and religious authority. Americans were horrified. The Communist Revolution in Russia in 1917 had raised fears of terrorist conspiracies, and incidents such as mail bombs intended for prominent Americans in 1919 convinced everyone that Communists and anarchists were real threats. Because Sacco and Vanzetti were anarchists as well as immigrants, they were seen as guilty from the beginning.

The two men went on trial on May 31, 1921, before Judge Webster Thayer, who was heard referring to the defendants as "those anarchist bastards"[160] during the course of the proceedings. Neither suspect had a criminal record, however, and neither seemed to be violent despite his political convictions. (Both men were, in fact, pacifists.) Sacco's employer described him as "a man who is in his garden

Italians Nicola Sacco (right) and Bartolomeo Vanzetti are led through a crowd in handcuffs after their arrest for robbery and murder. Despite solid alibis, the men were convicted and executed for the crimes.

at four o'clock in the morning and at the factory at seven o'clock and in his garden again after supper . . . carrying water and raising vegetables."[161] Vanzetti, an intellectual, stated in court, "Not only have I never committed a real crime in my life . . . I struggled all my life to eliminate crimes [including] the exploitation and the oppression of man by man."[162]

The testimony of a number of witnesses placed Sacco and Vanzetti far from South Braintree at the time of the murder. Nevertheless, the jury found both men guilty. They were sentenced to death. After a long series of unsuccessful appeals, they were executed on August 22, 1927. Not until fifty years later did Governor Michael Dukakis of Massachu-

setts clear the two men's names and acknowledge the flaws of the trial. He called on Americans to "resolve to prevent the forces of intolerance, fear, and hatred from ever again uniting to overcome rationality, wisdom, and fairness to which our legal system aspires."[163]

White Supremacy

The nation's intolerant attitude toward minorities was not only conveyed by the injustices of the Sacco-Vanzetti case. It was also expressed by the popularity of the Ku Klux Klan, which became extraordinarily powerful between 1920 and 1925.

At the height of their power, forty thousand members of the Ku Klux Klan parade down Pennsylvania Avenue in Washington, D.C.

The Klan was a secret terrorist organization with its roots in the Civil War. It had faded into obscurity until William Joseph Simmons, a former Methodist preacher, established a reorganized version of it in about 1915. Simmons called his new Klan the "Invisible Empire, Knights of the Ku Klux Klan." As with the original organization, Klan membership was open only to white, native-born Protestant men. However, by 1921, women were allowed to join as well.

The original Klan had focused on intimidating blacks, but the new Klan broadened its scope to target all minorities, including Catholics and Jews. The Klan claimed to cherish American values, but its appreciation was limited. One man explained,

The Klan taught the sanctity of the home. They wanted prayer in school. They wanted you to follow the Bible as long as you didn't admit that any part of it was Jewish. The Klan was very patriotic. And you were never to have anything to do with drink or loose women, even though most Klansmen would wink at each other on those issues.[164]

In time, the Klan became a kind of moral police force. In small towns in particular, members went on "night rides" to drive prostitutes out of town and close down gambling halls and speakeasies. There were thousands of instances of whippings and threats of whippings, especially in the South and Southwest, where the Klan was most ruthless.

Klan members dealt out punishments for the mildest of infringements. They threatened teens who were caught necking. They beat a man suspected of burglary until he confessed. They whipped, then tarred and feathered, a lawyer who accepted what they considered to be the wrong kind of clients. And whippings were not the worst that could happen. In at least one instance in Oklahoma, a black man was lynched after he failed to leave town before sundown.

While all this was going on, police often looked the other way either out of fear or sympathy. One man remembered, "On parade nights the traffic patrolmen disappeared, and traffic control was taken over by sheeted figures whose size and shape resembled those of the vanished patrolmen."[165]

"Us Against Them"

The Klan's moral stand, secret rituals, and dramatic white robes were highly appealing to poor and ignorant Americans who needed someone to blame for their poverty and powerlessness. One former member remembered, "The hatred was big. . . . We felt like we were just engulfed in a sea of people who were not us and [we] had to fight back."[166]

In the early 1920s, membership in the Klan rose dramatically. Numbers were highest in the South; they were also high in Indiana, Colorado, Oregon, California, Illinois, Ohio, Pennsylvania, and New Jersey. By 1924, national membership was estimated at 4 million, and several prominent politicians were Klan members. "Every businessman who was not Jewish belonged to the Klan, not necessarily because they believed in what the Klan said but because it was good business," one member stated, remembering conditions in his hometown. "Most ministers belonged to

the Klan. Many teachers belonged to the Klan."[167]

Not everyone was deceived by the Klan's patriotic and moral claims. Some people even took a strong stand against the Klan's attempts to establish itself in their midst. Immigrants in Pennsylvania's coal and steel towns broke up Klan meetings with clubs, fists, and guns. In a coal town in Illinois, there were shootouts in the streets between anti-Klan townspeople and Klan members who had come in to close the brothels and speakeasies. In New Jersey, six thousand supporters of local Jews and Catholics attacked Klan members, stoning, kicking, and beating them until they ran.

Nevertheless, Klan power grew until about 1925. That year, David C. Stephenson, the head of the Indiana Klan, began his drive to get the nomination to become the state's next senator. Stephenson's confidence was based on the fact that he had recently gotten a Klan-backed candidate elected as governor using colorful rhetoric that appealed to the voters' emotions. He hoped to achieve success using the same tactics:

> Remember, every criminal, every gambler, thug, libertine, girl-ruiner, home-wrecker, wife-beater, dope peddler, moonshiner, crooked politician, pagan papist [Catholic] priest, shyster lawyer, . . . white-slaver, brothel madam, Rome-controlled newspaper, black spider is fighting the Klan. Think it over—which side are you on?[168]

Despite his antivice oratory, however, Stephenson was vicious and unprincipled. In March 1925, he kidnapped and brutally attacked an Indiana state worker, Marge Oberholtzer, who had refused his sexual advances. To escape Stephenson's assault, Oberholtzer swallowed poison in an attempt to commit

The Appeal of the Klan

Most Americans saw the Ku Klux Klan as a dangerous terrorist organization, but others were attracted by its emphasis on patriotism and family values. Geoffrey Perrett describes the innocuous side of the Klan and its appeal in his book *America in the Twenties: A History*.

"For many, the Klan was still a fraternal organization, the only one they ever joined. The regalia, rituals, and camaraderie attracted more people than the chance of flogging somebody. Klan parades were a release from the dreariness of small-town life before radio helped occupy the evenings. The Klan, like radio, appealed to people whose imaginative needs were limited but unsatisfied. And there were the Klan picnics, boat trips, debating contests, spelling bees, and sightseeing tours. The large numbers of Pennsylvania Dutch (a corruption of Deutsch) who joined the Klan held sauerkraut dinners and goat roasts. A typical Klan ceremony involved entire families, drawn by fireworks, bands, a barbeque, hymn-singing, and setting fire to a forty-foot cross.

The ordinary Klansman wore a robe and a hood of white cotton; Klan officers . . . dressed in satin robes of brilliant colors, lavishly embroidered with silk. And what a sensation they caused on a Friday night in some drab little town when they paraded holding blazing torches. A Klan parade passed by in utter silence, a silence so complete, some claimed, that you could almost hear the breathing of the crowd."

The Ku Klux Klan performs an initiation ceremony.

Klan leader David C. Stephenson received a life sentence for the vicious kidnapping and attack of Marge Oberholtzer.

suicide. Stephenson returned her to her home, where she managed to tell her story to officials before she died. Her kidnapper was arrested, tried, and sentenced to life in prison. When the governor of Indiana refused to pardon him, Stephenson revealed information that sent several prominent officials to jail.

After the Stephenson scandal, most Americans saw the Klan for what it really was—an organization whose leadership preached morality while being lawless and morally corrupt. That realization shattered the faith of many members who were decent, hardworking citizens. The Klan's influence waned dramatically, and by 1928 it was a spent force. One former Klan member remembered, "People became disillusioned, is all I can say. We suddenly realized that those people, whom we had built up to hero status, not only had feet of clay, they had legs of clay. And it was a good riddance."[169]

New Channels

By the time Americans were saying "good riddance" to the Klan, the decade was drawing to a close. It had been characterized by more highs and lows than a roller coaster ride, but a final downturn was still to come. As one author notes, "Americans were soon to find themselves living in an altered world which called for new adjustments, new ideas, new habits of thought, and a new order of values. The psychological climate was changing; the ever-shifting currents of American life were turning into new channels."[170]

The razzle-dazzle twenties, the era that had roared so loud, would come to an end with an earthshaking crash.

The Crash

The excitement of the Roaring Twenties was still strong as the nation entered 1929. There were signs that the good times might be coming to an end, although no one envisioned they might end in a devastating crash. Wages had not gone up fast enough to cover the credit bills that everyone needed to pay off. Some people were cutting back on their spending. With goods that could not be sold, factories reduced production and laid off employees who then had no wages to spend. In a vicious cycle, the economy slowed. One banker told an investor, "Stocks look dangerously high to me. . . . Business is none too good. Of course if you buy the right stock you'll probably be all right in the long run and you may even make a profit. But if I were you I'd wait awhile and see what happens."[171]

The Great Bull Market

The public was not listening. Prosperity had lasted for so long, they could not believe it would soon end. Their optimism was driven by their unshakable confidence in business and by what became known as the Great Bull Market of 1928 and 1929.

The Great Bull Market grew out of the popularity of investing. The stock market seemed to be a veritable moneymaking machine. Everyone knew someone—their barber or their maid—who had "made a killing" by turning a few thousand dollars into a small fortune. People who had no money borrowed so they could buy. Even conservatives moved their life savings from banks to the stock market. One observer points out, "wives were asking their husbands why they were so slow, why they weren't getting in on all this, only to hear that their husbands had bought a hundred shares of American Linseed that very morning."[172]

Many people did not know all the ins and outs of investing wisely, but they believed that they knew enough to take the risk. As one historian writes, it seemed like everyone was "engaged in an exciting, profitable, and mysterious kind of transaction from which it was dull and stupid to be excluded."[173] Thus, the number of transactions and the value of stocks increased sharply as the decade wore on. About 220 million shares were traded in 1920, and over 1 billion in 1929. The Dow Jones Industrial Average (a measure of the value of several major stocks) stood at 95.11 in November 1922 and had quadrupled to 376.18 in August 1929.

By 1929, greed and overconfidence had pushed trading to the point of frenzy. Volumes increased from an average of 2 or 3 million shares traded daily to days when 6 million shares were bought and sold. And then the bubble burst. In September, prices reached an all-time high, only to drop sharply. Investors' confidence was shaken, and they began selling their shares. As the selling trend continued into October, panic set in. People who had been buying on credit decided they should get out while the getting was good, even if they had to take a loss.

On Black Thursday, October 24, more than 12 million shares were traded, and prices plummeted. At the end of the day, the *New York Times* reported that $4 billion had been lost. There was a brief upswing, and then on Tuesday, October 29, the market lost billions more with a record 16 million shares traded. One woman remembered, "Almost overnight it was like a bomb had fallen. All of the sudden, faces were tragic, and people were walking around in the hallways of our building and in the streets, with inquiring eyes saying, 'Has it happened to you?' It was awful."[174]

The days of prosperity were over. Businesses failed. Banks closed. People who had invested in the stock market suddenly realized that their savings had been wiped out. Their jobs were gone. They could not make payments on furniture, homes, or land, and so were forced to sell or forfeit. "It was like a domino effect: everything that happened to one person gradually happened to other people who were connected with them until everything just shut down,"[175] one person said. The Great Depression, a crushing blow to millions who had believed that if they worked hard enough they would be guaranteed success, lasted throughout the next decade. It ended only when the nation began gearing up for World War II.

A huge crowd gathers outside the New York Stock Exchange following the stock market crash in 1929. The crash brought an end to a decade of prosperity and ushered in the Great Depression.

Down, Down, Down

October 24, 1929, will forever be remembered as Black Thursday, the day that panic selling set the stock market tumbling to record losses. In *Only Yesterday: An Informal History of the 1920's*, historian Frederick Lewis Allen describes the hysteria that marked that memorable day.

"As the price structure crumbled there was a sudden stampede to get out from under. By eleven o'clock traders on the floor of the Stock Exchange were in a wild scramble to 'sell at the market.' Long before the lagging ticker could tell what was happening, word had gone out by telephone and telegraph that the bottom was dropping out of things, and the selling orders redoubled in volume. The leading stocks were going down two, three, and even five points between sales. Down, down, down. . . . Where were the bargain-hunters who were supposed to come to the rescue in times like this? Where were the investment trusts, which were expected to provide a cushion for the market by making new purchases at low prices? Where were the big operators who had declared that they were still bullish? Where were the powerful bankers who were supposed to be able at any moment to support prices? There seemed to be no support whatever. Down, down, down. The roar of voices which rose from the floor of the Exchange had become a roar of panic."

End of the Noble Experiment

The nation's reckless and rebellious spirit died away as people focused on survival. It was time to get serious, to somehow get the country back on track. That included dealing with Prohibition. The "drys" still insisted that the noble experiment was a success. Statistics, they said, showed that consumption of alcohol had declined during the decade. They also insisted that the nation's prosperity had been linked to Prohibition. If the ban on liquor was lifted, money that would normally be spent on consumer goods could be squandered on liquor.

The "wets" reacted to these arguments with scorn. Prohibition was a failure. There was more organized crime, more immorality, and more drunks on the street. Black Thursday had shown everyone how precarious the economy was. It was time to acknowledge the mistake of Prohibition and correct it. "Drink what you please, when you please," one wet wrote to express his point of view. "Urge others to drink. . . . In every way possible flaunt your defiance of the Eighteenth Amendment. Render it inoperative; ignore it, abrogate [repeal] it, wipe it out."[176]

Ordinary people were inclined to favor the wet argument. Prohibition had turned out to be more trouble than it was worth. Not only was the law unenforceable, but it was depriving people of jobs and the government of tax revenue at a time when every job and every dollar was vital. Will Rogers explained America's new reasoning when he said, "What does prohibition amount to, if your neighbor's children are not eating? . . . food, not drink is our problem now."[177]

Congress passed the Twenty-first Amendment repealing Prohibition at the end of 1933. That year, newly elected president Franklin Delano Roosevelt took office. His inauguration was a bright spot in a grim new era in

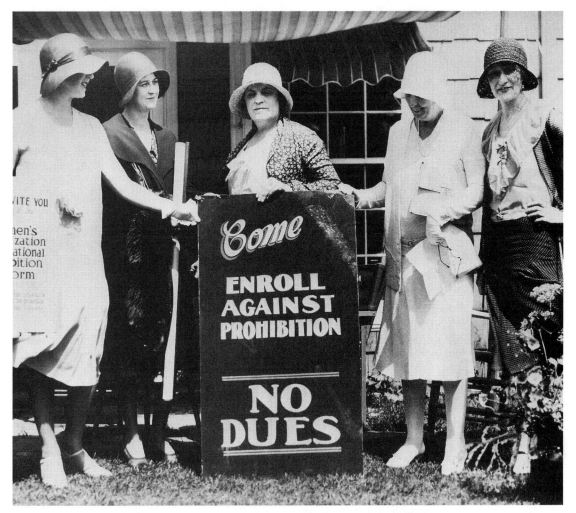

Women campaign against Prohibition in 1930. Prohibition was viewed largely as a failure and was officially ended by the Twenty-first Amendment in 1933.

which desperate Americans looked to strong leadership for reassurance and recovery.

The '20s Run Out

The Roaring Twenties had run out, ending in disaster. Few could say, however, that the era of silk stockings, bathtub gin, and hot jazz had been entirely frivolous. It had been a time when Americans expressed their frustration and naiveté after World War I. It had been a time when old habits and thought patterns had been challenged. Old ways of looking at politics, religion, marriage, morality, and public welfare had been evaluated and reshaped.

The '20s had ushered in the modern age for millions of Americans, most of whom would tell their children and grandchildren

The Crash Hits Home

It took time for Americans to realize that the stock market crash marked an end to the prosperity of the twenties. In his book *These Were Our Years*, author Frank Brookhouser remembers the moment his family faced the fact that times had changed.

"Wall Street was a long way from my home town but when it laid its egg, as the famous *Variety* headline said, the effects were felt in my town and every town, city, village, and hamlet in the land.

In time, the people in my town began to worry about one of the banks and, as it turned out, their fears were justified.

One evening when my father came home from work he was unusually quiet.

My mother could always sense when something was wrong, simply by the expression on my father's face. They had gone through a lot together and they knew each other very well.

'Is something wrong?' she asked this evening as she brought the dishes of food into the dining room from the kitchen.

My father looked up out of a downcast face. . . . 'The bank is closed,' he said slowly, softly.

'We'll lose our savings?' my mother asked.

'I'm afraid so.'

And my mother's expression became downcast, too, and she suddenly seemed weary. Those savings had been hard-earned and hard-saved.

'There is no use of worrying about it. After all, we haven't lost everything. We'll get along. . . .'

A lot of people were going to have to get along, somehow, during the decade after the Crash."

about the good times and play down the bad. One observer predicted, "Soon the mists of distance would soften the outlines of the nineteen-twenties and men and women . . . would smile at the memory of those charming, crazy days when the radio was a thrilling novelty, and girls wore bobbed hair and knee-length skirts, and a transatlantic flyer became a god overnight. . . . They would talk about the good old days."[178]

The Lawless Decade, the Flapper Era, the Jazz Age—the 1920s would never return, but their colorful legacy would never be forgotten.

Notes

Introduction: Age of Extremes

1. Quoted in Ezra Bowen, ed., *This Fabulous Century: 1920–1930*. New York: Time-Life Books, 1969, p. 49.
2. Robert S. and Helen Merrell Lynd, *Middletown: A Study in Contemporary American Culture*. New York: Harcourt Brace, 1929, p. 98.
3. Lynd, *Middletown*, p. 470.
4. Quoted in George Soule, *Prosperity Decade: From War to Depression, 1917–1929*. New York: Rinehart, 1947, p. 292.
5. Quoted in Laurence Bergreen, *Capone: The Man and the Era*. New York: Simon and Schuster, 1994, p. 83.
6. Quoted in Lynd, *Middletown*, p. 234.
7. Quoted in Lynd, *Middletown*, p. 143.
8. Ernest R. May, ed., *The Life History of the United States*. Vol. 10. New York: Time-Life Books, 1964, p. 119.
9. Kevin Rayburn, "The 1920s," 2000. www.louisville.edu/~kprayb01/1920s.html.

Chapter 1: Crazy Consumption

10. Quoted in Frederick Lewis Allen, *Only Yesterday: An Informal History of the 1920's*. 1931. Reprint, New York: Harper and Row, 1959, p. 35.
11. Quoted in Isabel Leighton, ed., *The Aspirin Age*. New York: Simon and Schuster, 1949, p. 147.
12. Quoted in Lynd, *Middletown*, p. 251.
13. Quoted in George E. Mowry, ed., *The Twenties: Fords, Flappers, and Fanatics*. Englewood Cliffs, NJ: Prentice-Hall, 1963, p. 49.
14. Quoted in Lynd, *Middletown*, p. 257.
15. Quoted in Marc McCutcheon, *The Writer's Guide to Everyday Life from Prohibition Through World War II*. Cincinnati, OH: Writer's Digest Books, 1995, p. 148.
16. Quoted in McCutcheon, *The Writer's Guide to Everyday Life from Prohibition Through World War II*, p. 149.
17. Quoted in McCutcheon, *The Writer's Guide to Everyday Life from Prohibition Through World War II*, p. 149.
18. Quoted in May, *The Life History of the United States*, p. 73.
19. Soule, *Prosperity Decade*, p. 169.
20. Quoted in Bowen, *This Fabulous Century*, p. 273.
21. Quoted in Lynd, *Middletown*, p. 88.
22. Lynd, *Middletown*, p. 46.
23. Quoted in Bowen, *This Fabulous Century*, p. 99.
24. Quoted in Bowen, *This Fabulous Century*, p. 99.
25. Lynd, *Middletown*, p. 45.
26. Allen, *Only Yesterday*, p. 138.
27. Quoted in Bowen, *This Fabulous Century*, p. 115.
28. Quoted in William E. Leuchtenburg, *The Perils of Prosperity, 1914–32*. Chicago: University of Chicago Press, 1958, p. 189.
29. Quoted in Mowry, *The Twenties*, p. 29.
30. Quoted in Lynd, *Middletown*, p. 350.
31. Quoted in Lynd, *Middletown*, p. 304.
32. Quoted in Lynd, *Middletown*, p. 47.
33. Quoted in Peter Jennings and Todd Brewster, *The Century*. New York: Doubleday Dell, 1998, p. 111.
34. Quoted in Lynd, *Middletown*, p. 173.
35. Quoted in Bowen, *This Fabulous Century*, pp. 268–69.

36. *Ladies Home Journal*, July 1925, p. 47.

37. *Ladies Home Journal*, July 1925, p. 70.

38. Quoted in Leuchtenburg, *The Perils of Prosperity, 1914–32*, p. 242.

39. Loren Baritz, ed., *The Culture of the Twenties*. New York: Bobbs-Merrill, 1970, pp. xxiii–xxiv.

Chapter 2: Thoroughly Modern

40. Quoted in Bergreen, *Capone*, p. 245.

41. Quoted in Lynd, *Middletown*, p. 151.

42. Quoted in Jennings and Brewster, *The Century*, p. 114.

43. Quoted in Lynd, *Middletown*, p. 29.

44. Quoted in Lynd, *Middletown*, p. 437.

45. Quoted in Lynd, *Middletown*, p. 156.

46. Quoted in Leuchtenburg, *The Perils of Prosperity, 1914–32*, pp. 172–73.

47. Allen, *Only Yesterday*, p. 82.

48. Quoted in Geoffrey Perrett, *America in the Twenties: A History*. New York: Simon and Schuster, 1982, p. 153.

49. Quoted in Jules Abels, *In the Time of Silent Cal: A Retrospective History of the 1920s*. New York: G.P. Putnam's Sons, 1969, p. 84.

50. Quoted in Lynd, *Middletown*, p. 128.

51. Quoted in Allen, *Only Yesterday*, p. 95.

52. Quoted in Elizabeth Stevenson, *Babbitts and Bohemians: The American 1920s*. New York: Macmillan, 1967, p. 155.

53. Quoted in Perrett, *America in the Twenties*, p. 149.

54. Quoted in Frank Freidel and Alan Brinkley, *America in the Twentieth Century*. New York: Alfred A. Knopf, 1982, p. 177.

55. Quoted in Lynd, *Middletown*, p. 49.

56. Quoted in Lynd, *Middletown*, p. 218.

57. Quoted in Lynd, *Middletown*, p. 137.

58. Quoted in Lynd, *Middletown*, p. 162.

59. Quoted in Lynd, *Middletown*, p. 161.

60. Quoted in Lynd, *Middletown*, p. 131.

61. Quoted in Jennings and Brewster, *The Century*, p. 142.

62. Quoted in Bowen, *This Fabulous Century*, p. 30.

63. Bruce Bliven, "Flapper Jane," *New Republic*, September 9, 1925. www.geocities. com/flapper_culture/jane.html.

64. Allen, *Only Yesterday*, pp. 73–74.

65. Quoted in May, *The Life History of the United States*, p. 107.

66. Quoted in Lynd, *Middletown*, p. 140.

67. Quoted in McCutcheon, *The Writer's Guide to Everyday Life from Prohibition Through World War II*, pp. 168–69.

68. Allen, *Only Yesterday*, p. 87.

69. Allen, *Only Yesterday*, p. 90.

70. Quoted in Bowen, *This Fabulous Century*, p. 30.

71. Quoted in Freidel and Brinkley, *America in the Twentieth Century*, p. 185.

72. Stevenson, *Babbitts and Bohemians*, p. 169.

73. May, *The Life History of the United States*, p. 141.

Chapter 3: Wonderful Nonsense

74. Quoted in Mowry, *The Twenties*, p. 46.

75. Quoted in Lynd, *Middletown*, p. 270.

76. Quoted in McCutcheon, *The Writer's Guide to Everyday Life from Prohibition Through World War II*, p. 181.

77. Jennings and Brewster, *The Century*, p. 110.

78. Quoted in Bowen, *This Fabulous Century*, p. 193.

79. Quoted in Leuchtenburg, *The Perils of Prosperity, 1914–32*, p. 168.

80. Quoted in Lynd, *Middletown*, p. 266.

81. Quoted in Lynd, *Middletown*, p. 265.

82. Quoted in John K. Hutchens and George Oppenheimer, eds., *The Best in The World*. New York: Viking Press, 1973, p. 243.

83. Quoted in Jennings and Brewster, *The Century*, p. 129.
84. Quoted in Abels, *In the Time of Silent Cal*, p. 191.
85. Quoted in Richard M. Ketchum, *Will Rogers: The Man and His Times*. New York: American Heritage, 1973, p. 280.
86. "Nation Hears Story of Byrd Welcome," *New York Times*, June 20, 1930, p. 2.
87. Quoted in Mowry, *The Twenties*, p. 82.
88. Quoted in Bowen, *This Fabulous Century*, p. 63.
89. Quoted in Frank Brookhouser, ed., *These Were Our Years: A Panoramic and Nostalgic Look at American Life Between the Two World Wars*. New York: Doubleday, 1959, p. 291.
90. Quoted in Leighton, *The Aspirin Age*, p. 168.
91. Quoted in "Famous Words About the Babe," Babe Ruth website, 2000. www.baberuth.com/quote2a.html.
92. Quoted in Mowry, *The Twenties*, p. 70.
93. Quoted in Bowen, *This Fabulous Century*, p. 240.
94. Quoted in McCutcheon, *The Writer's Guide to Everyday Life from Prohibition Through World War II*, p. 217.
95. Quoted in McCutcheon, *The Writer's Guide to Everyday Life from Prohibition Through World War II*, pp. 217–18.
96. Quoted in Bowen, *This Fabulous Century*, p. 248.
97. Quoted in Bowen, *This Fabulous Century*, p. 243.
98. Quoted in Bowen, *This Fabulous Century*, p. 244.
99. Quoted in Perrett, *America in the Twenties*, p. 234.
100. Quoted in Jennings and Brewster, *The Century*, p. 135.
101. Quoted in Anne Shaw Faulkner, "Does Jazz Put the Sin in Syncopation?" *Ladies Home Journal*, August 1921, p. 16.
102. Quoted in Bowen, *This Fabulous Century*, p. 91.
103. Langston Hughes, *The Simple Omnibus*. 1961. Reprint, Mattituck, NY: Aeionian Press, 1978, p. 30.

Chapter 4: "Goodbye, John Barleycorn"

104. Quoted in Abels, *In the Time of Silent Cal*, p. 89.
105. Quoted in Andrew Sinclair, *Prohibition: The Era of Excess*. Boston: Little, Brown, 1962, p. 63.
106. Quoted in Mowry, *The Twenties*, p. 91.
107. Quoted in Bowen, *This Fabulous Century*, p. 154.
108. Betty DeRamus, "Prohibition: Liquor and Lawlessness," *Detroit News*, May 31, 2001. www.detnews.com/history/river300/0531/0531.htm.
109. Quoted in Everett S. Allen, *The Black Ships: Rumrunners of Prohibition*. Boston: Little, Brown, 1979, p. 31.
110. Quoted in Mowry, *The Twenties*, p. 97.
111. Quoted in Sinclair, *Prohibition*, p. 202.
112. Quoted in Sinclair, *Prohibition*, p. 207.
113. Quoted in Herbert Asbury, *The Great Illusion: An Informal History of Prohibition*. New York: Doubleday, 1950, p. 272. www.hoboes.com/html/Politics/Prohibition/Notes/Illusion.html#Heading11.
114. Quoted in Asbury, *The Great Illusion*, p. 286.
115. Quoted in McCutcheon, *The Writer's Guide to Everyday Life from Prohibition Through World War II*, p. 51.
116. Quoted in McCutcheon, *The Writer's Guide to Everyday Life from Prohibition Through World War II*, p. 45.
117. Quoted in Brookhouser, *These Were Our Years*, pp. 120–21.

118. Quoted in Stevenson, *Babbitts and Bohemians*, p. 146.
119. Quoted in Leo Trachtenberg, "Texas Guinan: Queen of the Night," *Urbanities*, Spring 1998. www.city-journal.org/html/8_2_urbanities-texas.html.
120. Quoted in Robert J. Schoenberg, *Mr. Capone*. New York: William Morrow, 1992, p. 288.
121. Asbury, *The Great Illusion*, p. 167.
122. Quoted in McCutcheon, *The Writer's Guide to Everyday Life from Prohibition Through World War II*, p. 44.
123. Quoted in Mowry, *The Twenties*, p. 108.
124. Quoted in Leighton, *The Aspirin Age*, p. 48.
125. Quoted in Bowen, *This Fabulous Century*, p. 166.
126. Quoted in Marilyn Bardsley, "Eliot Ness: The Man Behind the Myth," *Crime Library*, 2001. www.crimelibrary.com/ness/nessuntouch.htm.
127. Quoted in McCutcheon, *The Writer's Guide to Everyday Life from Prohibition Through World War II*, p. 43.

Chapter 5: Outside the Law

128. Stevenson, *Babbitts and Bohemians*, p. 143.
129. Quoted in Perrett, *America in the Twenties*, p. 357.
130. Quoted in Mowry, *The Twenties*, p. 34.
131. Quoted in Perrett, *America in the Twenties*, p. 360.
132. Perrett, *America in the Twenties*, p. 361.
133. Quoted in Bergreen, *Capone*, p. 268.
134. Bergreen, *Capone*, p. 19.
135. Quoted in Bergreen, *Capone*, p. 368.
136. Allen, *Only Yesterday*, p. 217.
137. Quoted in Schoenberg, *Mr. Capone*, p. 160.
138. Quoted in Bergreen, *Capone*, p. 79.
139. Bergreen, *Capone*, p. 225.
140. Quoted in "Al Capone," *Crime Library*, 2001. www.crimelibrary.com/capone/caponepublic.htm.
141. Quoted in Hutchens and Oppenheimer, *The Best in* The World, p. 268.
142. Quoted in Bowen, *This Fabulous Century*, p. 198.
143. Quoted in Robert Grant and Joseph Katz, *The Great Trials of the Twenties: The Watershed Decade in America's Courtrooms*. Rockville Centre, NY: Sarpedon, 1998, p. 184.
144. Quoted in Grant and Katz, *The Great Trials of the Twenties*, p. 185.
145. Quoted in Grant and Katz, *The Great Trials of the Twenties*, p. 185.
146. Quoted in Grant and Katz, *The Great Trials of the Twenties*, p. 187.
147. Quoted in Hutchens and Oppenheimer, *The Best in* The World, p. 148.
148. Quoted in Grant and Katz, *The Great Trials of the Twenties*, p. 194.

Chapter 6: The Monkey Trial and the Invisible Empire

149. Lynd, *Middletown*, p. 479.
150. Lynd, *Middletown*, p. 315.
151. Quoted in Lynd, *Middletown*, pp. 376–77.
152. William Ashley (Billy) Sunday, "Quotes and Notes," *Wholesome Words*, 2001. www.wholesomewords.org/echoes/sunday.html.
153. Quoted in "The McPherson-Bogard Debate: On Miraculous Divine Healing," May 22, 1934. www.padfield.com/acrobat/bogard.pdf.
154. Quoted in Hutchens and Oppenheimer, *The Best in* The World, p. 359.
155. "A Thunderous Welcome," *New York Times*, June 28, 1926, p. 2.
156. Quoted in Leuchtenburg, *The Perils of Prosperity, 1914–32*, p. 221.

157. Quoted in Grant and Katz, *The Great Trials of the Twenties*, p. 154.
158. Allen, *Only Yesterday*, p. 169.
159. Quoted in Grant and Katz, *The Great Trials of the Twenties*, p. 161.
160. Quoted in Leuchtenburg, *The Perils of Prosperity, 1914–32*, p. 82.
161. Quoted in Grant and Katz, *The Great Trials of the Twenties*, p. 26.
162. Quoted in Grant and Katz, *The Great Trials of the Twenties*, p. 27.
163. Michael S. Dukakis, *A Proclamation*, July 19, 1977. www.saccovanzettiproject. org/pages/dukakis.html.
164. Quoted in Jennings and Brewster, *The Century*, p. 120.
165. Quoted in Leighton, *The Aspirin Age*, p. 115.
166. Quoted in Jennings and Brewster, *The Century*, p. 120.
167. Quoted in Jennings and Brewster, *The Century*, p. 120.
168. Quoted in Abels, *In the Time of Silent Cal*, p. 57.
169. Quoted in Jennings and Brewster, *The Century*, p. 120.
170. Allen, *Only Yesterday*, p. 281.

Chapter 7: The Crash

171. Quoted in Allen, *Only Yesterday*, p. 241.
172. Allen, *Only Yesterday*, p. 247.
173. Stevenson, *Babbitts and Bohemians*, p. 228.
174. Quoted in Jennings and Brewster, *The Century*, p. 150.
175. Quoted in Jennings and Brewster, *The Century*, p. 150.
176. Quoted in Sinclair, *Prohibition*, p. 370.
177. Quoted in Sinclair, *Prohibition*, p. 394.
178. Allen, *Only Yesterday*, pp. 296–97.

For Further Reading

Linda Jacobs Altman, *The Decade That Roared: America During Prohibition*. New York: Henry Holt, 1997. A very good account of the 1920s with an emphasis on Prohibition.

Fon W. Boardman Jr., *America and the Jazz Age: A History of the 1920s*. New York: Henry Z. Walck, 1968. Another very good account of the Roaring Twenties.

Martin Hintz, *Farewell, John Barleycorn: Prohibition in the United States*. Minneapolis, MN: Lerner Publications, 1996. Discusses Prohibition and its consequences in the United States.

Edmund Lindop, *Dazzling Twenties*. New York: Franklin Watts, 1970. Good overview of the 1920s.

Tom McGowen, *The Great Monkey Trial: Science vs. Fundamentalism in America*. New York: Franklin Watts, 1990. An account of the Scopes trial that pitted modern science against fundamentalism.

David Pietrusza, *The Roaring Twenties*. San Diego, CA: Lucent Books, 1998. An examination of all aspects of the 1920s, including Prohibition, presidential scandals, fads, controversies, and the stock market crash. Includes many good primary and secondary source quotes.

Bill Severn, *The End of the Roaring Twenties: Prohibition and Repeal*. New York: Julian Messner, 1969. A complete account of Prohibition, including the roots of the anti-alcohol movement in the United States and the unprecedented repeal of the Eighteenth Amendment.

Works Consulted

Books

Jules Abels, *In the Time of Silent Cal: A Retrospective History of the 1920s*. New York: G.P. Putnam's Sons, 1969. An overview of America during President Calvin Coolidge's administration.

Everett S. Allen, *The Black Ships: Rumrunners of Prohibition*. Boston: Little, Brown, 1979. The story of the smuggling fleet that supplied liquor to America during Prohibition.

Frederick Lewis Allen, *Only Yesterday: An Informal History of the 1920's*. 1931. Reprint, New York: Harper and Row, 1959. One of the first histories written about the 1920s, drawn from documents, articles, and statistics of the era.

Loren Baritz, ed., *The Culture of the Twenties*. New York: Bobbs-Merrill, 1970. An anthology of work from authors, politicians, social critics, and personalities of the twenties. Includes excerpts written by Bartolomeo Vanzetti, Bruce Barton, F. Scott Fitzgerald, John Dewey, and many others.

Laurence Bergreen, *Capone: The Man and the Era*. New York: Simon and Schuster, 1994. Well-written biography of one of the most notorious gangsters of the 1920s. Includes a great deal of information about the era itself.

Ezra Bowen, ed., *This Fabulous Century: 1920–1930*. New York: Time-Life Books, 1969. A superior overview of the '20s, including dozens of period photos, advertising blurbs, tabloid articles, and other material.

Frank Brookhouser, ed., *These Were Our Years: A Panoramic and Nostalgic Look at American Life Between the Two World Wars*. New York: Doubleday, 1959. A collection of articles that reflects American life during the '20s. Covers Prohibition, the automobile industry, jazz, the Scopes trial, Lindbergh's flight, the sports craze, and the 1929 stock market crash.

Frank Freidel and Alan Brinkley, *America in the Twentieth Century*. New York: Alfred A. Knopf, 1982. A history of the twentieth century with emphasis on politics, economics, and social development. Includes a chapter on the 1920s.

Robert Grant and Joseph Katz, *The Great Trials of the Twenties: The Watershed Decade in America's Courtrooms*. Rockville Centre, NY: Sarpedon, 1998. A focused look at ten controversial trials of the 1920s, including those of Sacco and Vanzetti, Al Capone, Fatty Arbuckle, Klan leader David Stephenson, John Scopes, and Leopold and Loeb.

Langston Hughes, *The Simple Omnibus*. 1961. Reprint, Mattituck, NY: Aeionian Press, 1978. A collection of articles by one of the renowned black writers and poets of the 1920s.

John K. Hutchens and George Oppenheimer, eds., *The Best in* The World. New York: Viking Press, 1973. A selection of news and feature stories, editorials, humor, poems, and reviews included in *The World* newspaper.

Peter Jennings and Todd Brewster, *The Century*. New York: Doubleday Dell, 1998. A chronicle of the twentieth century by a renowned broadcast journalist and a former editor of *Life* magazine. A chapter on the '20s includes several first-person accounts of bootlegging, the Scopes trial, KKK activities, and others topics.

Richard M. Ketchum, *Will Rogers: The Man and His Times*. New York: American Heritage, 1973. Biography of the preeminent humorist from his birth to his tragic death in 1935. Includes an extensive collection of Will Rogers's sayings.

Isabel Leighton, ed., *The Aspirin Age*. New York: Simon and Schuster, 1949. A collection of articles focusing on such public figures as Izzy and Moe, Aimee Semple McPherson, Charles Lindbergh, Calvin Coolidge, Jack Dempsey, Gene Tunney, and others.

William E. Leuchtenburg, *The Perils of Prosperity, 1914–32*. Chicago: University of Chicago Press, 1958. A history of the 1920s tracing political, social, economic, and cultural changes during the era.

Robert S. and Helen Merrell Lynd, *Middletown: A Study in Contemporary American Culture*. New York: Harcourt Brace, 1929. An in-depth study of community life—homes, education, religious observances, changing values—in a typical midwestern town (Muncie, Indiana) in the 1920s.

Ernest R. May, ed., *The Life History of the United States*. Vol. 10. New York: Time-Life Books, 1964. Well-written overview of the '20s complete with period photos.

Marc McCutcheon, *The Writer's Guide to Everyday Life from Prohibition Through World War II*. Cincinnati, OH: Writer's Digest Books, 1995. The book contains a wide variety of fascinating information about life in the 1920s, including slang, clothing, music, cars, and crime.

George E. Mowry, ed., *The Twenties: Fords, Flappers, and Fanatics*. Englewood Cliffs, NJ: Prentice-Hall, 1963. An excellent collection of magazine excerpts, newspaper articles, and personal accounts taken from the 1920s. Covers the Florida land boom, the perils of credit buying, the mah-jongg and crossword puzzle craze, women smokers, and a host of other topics.

Geoffrey Perrett, *America in the Twenties: A History*. New York: Simon and Schuster, 1982. An in-depth look at the 1920s, including the changing role of women, the impact of jazz, the collapse of old ideals, and the rise of modern attitudes.

Robert J. Schoenberg, *Mr. Capone*. New York: William Morrow, 1992. A portrait of the most infamous gangster of the Roaring Twenties.

Andrew Sinclair, *Prohibition: The Era of Excess*. Boston: Little, Brown, 1962. The story of Prohibition with an emphasis on the personal aspects of the noble experiment.

George Soule, *Prosperity Decade: From War to Depression, 1917–1929*. New York: Rinehart, 1947. Covers the economic background of the 1920s and how it contributed to the excitement of the period.

Elizabeth Stevenson, *Babbitts and Bohemians: The American 1920s*. New York: Macmillan, 1967. Conveys the extremes of the twenties by giving an overview of the conformity and rebellion that marked the time.

Periodicals

Anne Shaw Faulkner, "Does Jazz Put the Sin in Syncopation?" *Ladies Home Journal*, August 1921. An article critical of jazz written by the national music chairperson of the General Federation of Women's Clubs of America.

"Nation Hears Story of Byrd Welcome," *New York Times*, June 20, 1930. Discusses radio networks that broadcast Admiral Richard E. Byrd's triumphant homecoming. Byrd became the first man to fly over the South Pole in 1929.

"A Thunderous Welcome," *New York Times*, June 28, 1926. Discusses evangelist Aimee Semple McPherson's return to the Angelus Temple after her mysterious disappearance in May 1926.

Internet Sources

Herbert Asbury, *The Great Illusion: An Informal History of Prohibition*. New York: Doubleday, 1950. www.hoboes.com/html/Politics/Prohibition/Notes/Illusion.html#Heading11. Excerpts from a book on Prohibition, written by an expert social historian.

Vivian M. Baulch, "How Billy Sunday Battled Demon Rum in Detroit," *Detroit News*, 2000. www.detroitnews.com/history/sunday/sunday.htm. A lengthy article on evangelist Billy Sunday's visit to Detroit in 1916.

Bruce Bliven, "Flapper Jane," *New Republic*, September 9, 1925. www.geocities.com/flapper_culture/jane.html. An article that details the lifestyle and outlook of a typical flapper.

Betty DeRamus, "Prohibition: Liquor and Lawlessness," *Detroit News*, May 31, 2001. www.detnews.com/history/river300/0531/0531.htm. A fascinating article about the "wet" city of Detroit, Michigan, during Prohibition.

"The McPherson-Bogard Debate: On Miraculous Divine Healing," May 22, 1934. www.padfield.com/acrobat/bogard.pdf. Details the debate between Baptist leader Dr. Ben M. Bogard and evangelist Aimee Semple McPherson.

Leo Trachtenberg, "Texas Guinan: Queen of the Night," *Urbanities*, Spring 1998. www.city-journal.org/html/8_2_urbanities-texas.html. A detailed article about the Queen of the Speakeasies, Tex Guinan.

Websites

Babe Ruth Website (www.baberuth.com). The official website of the Sultan of Swat.

Crime Library (www.crimelibrary.com). A website that covers classic crime stories, outlaws and gangsters, mass and serial murders, terrorists, spies, and assassins, and great crime fiction.

The 1920s (www.louisville.edu/~kprayb01/1920s.html). An excellent site focusing on the 1920s.

The Sacco-Vanzetti Project (www.saccovanzettiproject.org). This project aims to publicize the Sacco-Vanzetti case through a presentation of online visual materials, documents, a bibliography, and a chronology. Includes an e-mail address for those with questions.

Wholesome Words (www.wholesomewords.org). Provides information on the modern fundamentalist movement, Christian poetry, quotes from renowned Christian leaders, and other material.

Index

Picture Credits

Cover: ©Bettmann/CORBIS

©Bettmann/CORBIS, 10, 25, 26, 27, 30, 33, 41, 43, 47, 49, 50, 51, 52, 56, 62, 63, 66, 69, 70, 75, 78, 82, 91, 95

©Gehl Company/CORBIS, 21

Hulton/Archive by Getty Images, 9, 12, 13, 15, 16, 22, 36, 59, 71, 77, 81, 83, 85, 87, 88, 90

Library of Congress, 28, 34, 44, 46, 64, 93

©Minnesota Historical Society/CORBIS, 19, 55, 58

National Archives, 72

Smithsonian Institution, 39

Stock Montage, Inc., 17

About the Author

Diane Yancey works as a freelance writer in the Pacific Northwest, where she has lived for over twenty years. She writes nonfiction for middle-grade and high school readers and enjoys traveling and collecting old books. Some of her other books include *Life in the Elizabethan Theater, Life in Charles Dickens's England, Life in a Japanese American Internment Camp*, and *Life on the Pony Express*.